G000253560

UNDERSTANDING
THE ROYAL ARCH

Understanding
The Royal Arch

Including the addresses delivered to the annual
Convocations of the Province of
Northamptonshire and Huntingdonshire
during the period 1978-1990 when the author
was the ME Superintendent in and over the Province.

RICHARD S. E. SANDBACH

Lewis Masonic

First published 1992
Reprinted 1998
This impression 2003

ISBN 0 85318 193 4

All rights reserved. No part of this book may be reproduced or
transmitted in any form or by any means, electronic or
mechanical, including photocopying, recording or by any
information storage and retrieval system, without permission
from the Publisher in writing.

© Richard S. E. Sandbach 1992

Published by Lewis Masonic

an imprint of Ian Allan Publishing Ltd,
Hersham, Surrey KT12 4RG.
Printed by Ian Allan Printing Ltd,
Hersham, Surrey KT12 4RG.

British Library Cataloguing in Publication Data.
Sandbach, R. S. E.
Understanding the Royal Arch
1. title
366

DEDICATED
to
CLIFFORD ELLAM JONES, M.B.E.
Past Deputy G.Superintendent
and
BASIL REGINALD DIXON
Past Second Pr G Principal
Northamptonshire and Huntingdonshire
with
Affection and Gratitude
for their
Encouragement, support and Companionship

ACKNOWLEDGEMENTS

My grateful thanks and acknowledgements are given to the following for permission to reproduce letters and extracts in this book.

Board of General Purposes for reproducing the leaflet and extracts of text in Appendices A, C and D.

Church House Publishing for giving permission to reproduce the extracts from *Freemasonry and Christianity*, *Towards a Theology for Inter-Faith Dialogue* and *We Believe in God*.

The Rt. Rev. William Westwood, Lord Bishop of Peterborough for permission to quote from a most helpful letter to me.

CONTENTS

APPENDICES

ILLUSTRATIONS
(Between pages 50-51)

INTRODUCTION AND EXPLANATION

THIS IS A BOOK intended primarily for Freemasons who have joined a Chapter and so have become Royal Arch Companions. Because it includes addresses delivered annually over the period 1978-1990 comments on the attitudes of the Churches to Freemasonry and of Freemasonry to religion occur. In that sphere it is not my wish to stir controversy or even to try to modify the views of any critic of Freemasonry, but only to do my best to help Royal Arch Companions to clarify their thoughts about the Order and to understand what the critics are saying and, so far as possible, why they are saying it. The book is addressed to a masonic audience; if any who are opposed to or critical of Freemasonry read it I hope they will find it a sober, realistic and charitable exposition of the opposite view to their own and of the criticisms levelled against the Craft in recent years; but I do not expect and am not trying to alter their convictions.

Although Laurence Dermott[1] called the Holy Royal Arch 'the root, heart and marrow of Freemasonry' it is not until one has been a member for some time that the truth of this statement becomes apparent; for some it never does. I cannot claim to have thought deeply about the Order before becoming head of a Royal Arch Province in 1978 in which capacity I was expected to address the Companions of the Province of Northamptonshire & Huntingdonshire at the Annual Convocation. Thinking about what to say that might be constructive led to thinking seriously about the ethos of the Order.

At that time the standard answer to the question 'Why should I join Chapter?' was 'It completes the Third Degree and gives you the lost secrets'[2]. This never seemed very convincing and was even less so if one thought seriously about the Order. The title of the Order, 'The Supreme Order of the Holy Royal Arch' seemed to provide a good starting point and thinking about this led to a realisation that there was indeed much more to ponder; but would the Companions feel that such talks were worth listening to? Tentative (and to tell the truth rather nervous) experiment beginning in 1979 indicated that they did, and comments of visitors from other Provinces were encouraging. The 'speculative' element began to take over the whole address and though each one now took much longer to prepare, the result was rewarding for me and seemed to be helpful for others. As the years went by perhaps I began to glimpse what Dermott had meant.

A Freemason is enjoined from the start of his masonic career to think seriously about the purpose of life, and Royal Arch Chapters will only flourish and grow if Companions appreciate that there is purpose and meaning to the Order. Though ceremonial may attract interest it can rarely convert attention into understanding and so into enthusiasm.

When it was time to retire as ruler I was asked to consider bringing the addresses together. That was the origin of this book, of which they form the greater part. As they have been left on the whole very much in the form in which they were delivered they are direct in style rather than impersonal and show a development of thought rather than a settled philosophy; this however probably has the merit of brevity, since none lasted for longer then ten minutes.

The first two chapters and the last do not consist of addresses delivered in Provincial Chapter but they too originated as addresses, one to a Deanery Synod to whom I was asked to speak about Freemasonry following the debate on the subject in the General Synod of the Church of England in 1987, another on the history of the Royal Arch and the third on the historical background to the legend of the Order and some lessons we can draw from it. As each chapter is self-contained there is inevitably some duplication but it seemed preferable to allow this rather than damage the cohesion of each or make it more difficult for them to be read in Chapter if any Companion should desire to do so — in which case I hope his attention will be drawn to the 'Final Word' printed at the end of the book.

Storm clouds intruded into the progression as the media and the more extreme elements in the Churches began to attack Freemasonry. There were churchmen and churchgoers whose motives arose from genuine (though in our view misguided) disquiet, usually stated to be based on theological grounds; some laymen explained their attitude as expressing 'public concern' but often did not appear averse to reaping personal benefit from ventilating their views; some saw the Craft as wedded to the maintenance of a stable society which they wished for their own reasons to upset, and joyfully joined in the hunt; some were quite simply 'nutters'; and there were some whose motives were obscure, sometimes personal, sometimes claimed as grounded on principle, sometimes arising from some alleged masonic conspiracy the nature of which varied in accordance with the preconceptions or prejudices of the individual. It was a difficult time and rightly or wrongly I saw my duty as trying to help those for whom I was responsible to understand what was happening, to appreciate genuine concern where it existed, to keep a sense of proportion, and to work out what we should say to our critics in explaining our position. This proved to be an excellent personal discipline, but knowing by then that my terms of office would end in 1990 meant working to a final date; so the 1989 and 1990 addresses try to sum up what this pilgrimage has taught me so far. The journey is not yet complete and perhaps this book will inspire others to probe further.

In one matter above all others we have been very fortunate in Northamptonshire and Huntingdonshire, that is in having the support and understanding of so many of the clergy both at diocesan and parish level and among the non-conformist ministers. To all of them who have tried to understand and have listened with sympathy I offer our deepest gratitude. It was this element of understanding that led to the invitation to address the Deanery Synod and just as that paper had to start from scratch in introducing Freemasonry in the Province to a largely non-masonic audience this collection starts with an updated version in order that readers may appreciate the background against which each address was delivered.

There are of course several different methods of 'working' the Royal Arch. Some Companions may therefore find practices referred to which differ in detail from those to which they are accustomed; but the message and the teaching are the same in all and I hope for their indulgence.

[1] Laurence Dermott was the second Grand Secretary of the 'Antients' Grand Lodge, as to which see Chapter 2. This was the Grand Lodge which particularly sponsored the Royal Arch.

[2] Peterborough Booklet No 5, *Why Join The Royal Arch*, suggests a more satisfactory approach which is in conformity with the ideas in this book

1
THE CHURCH AND
FREEMASONRY (1988)

I have never made any attempt either to conceal my masonic interest or to evade serious questions about it. It was well known both to diocesan and parochial authorities and no criticism has been levelled against me on account of it either as chairman of the Diocesan Board of Finance for 10 years or as a sidesman in the parish church (a duty which many Freemasons seem to perform). I had been engaged in a certain amount of correspondence with Church authorities prior to the debate on Freemasonry in the General Synod, and in 1988 soon after it had taken place was invited to address the Peterborough Deanery Synod about the Craft. The following talk was the result. It provides a background for the thoughts developed in the later addresses. Figures etc have been updated in notes.

FOR MANY YEARS comment about Freemasonry, however ill-informed or even (as does unhappily sometimes happen) malicious, has been allowed to go unanswered; and while this has often meant that attacks crumbled for want of an adversary, in the long run each left debris which served as a bridgehead for the next set of attackers. Most philosophies and most religions have suffered similarly from time to time. The early Christian Church was no exception — for instance it was quite seriously accused of cannibalism by opponents who misunderstood its ceremonies. We have now decided it is time to clear the debris and speak for our principles.

It is important to realize that there are certain groups, particularly overseas, which call themselves masonic, but which we do not recognize as such and regard as irregular. The reason is that they do not conform to the standards for recognition accepted by English Freemasons and agreed by other Grand Lodges with whom we are, to use the technical term, 'in communication'. This is usually on one of three grounds. The first is a failure to require that an applicant for admission must affirm his belief in a Supreme Being before he can be accepted as a candidate. The second is a failure to require that a candidate shall take his Obligation on, or in full view of, the book or writing which he regards as binding on his conscience in accordance with his religion, and that it shall be open. In the English Constitution — that is, in all lodges subject to the United Grand Lodge of England whether at home or abroad, the Holy Bible must be open in Lodge in front of the Master while the Lodge is in session; if a Jewish or other non-Christian candidate is taking an Obligation then the book or writing regarded by his Faith as sacred will also be exhibited open where he can readily see it and if appropriate hold it. The third common reason for non-recognition is failure to insist that Freemasonry is non-political.

I am only going to talk about English Freemasonry as it is practised under the United Grand Lodge of England, which controls the three basic degrees, ('The Craft') and the Royal Arch or Chapter, an extension of the Craft. This of course excludes certain Orders referred to in the report of the General Synod's working party, notably the 'Ancient and Accepted Rite', Knights Templar and Order of the Red Cross of Constantine, all of which are Christian masonic Orders; but I am head only of the Craft and Royal Arch in this area and so not entitled to speak for others *ex cathedra.*

Within these parameters then the first question must be 'What is Freemasonry?' You have with your papers a leaflet about this published by the United Grand Lodge[1]. It tells you a great deal in a small space but I want to put flesh on the bones; so let us start with a recognized definition: 'Freemasonry is a system of morality'; the word 'morality' is used here in the sense (as given in the Concise Oxford Dictionary) of 'moral conduct (especially good)'. This is probably the most important point I shall make to you, because most serious criticism of the Craft from religious sources seems to be based on the groundless supposition that it is or aspires to be a religion[2].

Now a word about organization. The Grand Master, who is elected annually, has great power, but the United Grand Lodge is the actual governing body. Lodges outside London are grouped in Provinces, each under a Provincial Grand Master. We tend to stick to the old county boundaries so the Province which I rule is 'Northamptonshire and Huntingdonshire'; it comprises the old counties of those names. plus the Soke of Peterborough and Stamford, so that you will see it is largely coterminous with the diocese of Peterborough (omitting Rutland) but also includes parts of the dioceses of Ely and Lincoln. There are 66 lodges in the Province with three more on the stocks and rather over three and a half thousand men, a figure which is at present increasing by about 40 net each year[3]. In 1986 the Province admitted

138 men into the Craft[4]. Every year United Grand Lodge issues between 13,000 and 15,000 certificates to new members world-wide[5] and sanctions some 30 to 40 new lodges over the whole of the English Constitution.

As to qualifications for membership, we are always careful to find out why a man is coming forward, because we do not want anyone who seeks admission for (to quote the ritual) 'mercenary or other unworthy motive'; and a man who is accepted will be asked in Open Lodge before the ceremony proper begins to confirm that he is prompted to come forward by 'a favourable opinion preconceived of the Institution, a general desire of knowledge, and a sincere wish to render himself more extensively serviceable to his fellow-creatures'.

There would not be much point in all this if we did not have definite ideals and did not instruct brethren in them. The ground work will have been laid even before a man is proposed as a candidate when he meets the Lodge committee. At that meeting he will be asked to confirm his religious belief in a Supreme Being and informed that he will be expected to continue to practise the religion he professes once he is admitted.

He will also be told about the financial commitment, including the masonic duty to support charity; and if he is married he will be asked whether his wife and family support his candidature. He will be informed that he is required to take an oath to behave in accordance with our precepts and not to disclose secrets. He can ask questions about any of this, or anything else, and either answers or an explanation of why an answer is not forthcoming will be given. So he does know quite a lot about what is to happen and what is expected of him before he sets foot in the Lodge room. Then before he takes the Obligation he is assured that there is nothing in it incompatible with his civil, moral or religious duties.

Our critics are very good at seizing with derision or horror on parts of what they consider to be our rituals, often taking them out of context, and have been known to move the goalposts when it looked as though they might be losing. In fact, as you watch a ceremony unfold, even though you have heard it many times before, it has great fascination. Bear in mind that none of it is read and the performers usually change every year. Everything has to be learnt, and the dignity and order of a well-executed ceremony impress and satisfy not only the onlooker but also those taking part, including particularly the candidate, to whom each ceremony is designed to give a message. In a section of the First Degree ceremony which somehow never gets mentioned by the critics the principles of brotherly love and the necessity for harmony in the Lodge are emphasized, as also in a most vivid manner is the mason's duty to succour the needy and distressed. Finally, a long address, the Charge after Initiation, stresses that a Freemason is expected to do his duty to his God, to his neighbour and to himself. It is delivered orally to the candidate, often by a Brother whom he knows well and the fact that his friend has taken the trouble to learn all this on his behalf is something which always makes a great impression on the new Brother.

I have dwelt on this at some length for three reasons: first, to emphasize that a candidate in fact knows a great deal about what he is being asked to promise and to undertake; second, to show you that our critics tend to be rather selective and to take things out of context; and third, to point out that instruction in moral duties begins at the start of a man's masonic career.

Next, a word about the rituals. No supernatural origin is claimed for them. It is well known that they evolved over a long period and that all the versions now in general use came into existence in the years following 1813 when two rival Grand Lodges in London came together to form the United Grand Lodge of England under HRH the Duke of Sussex as Grand Master. He was a practising Christian, a noted Hebrew scholar and a keen Freemason who had thought profoundly about the ethos of the Craft and held that, as a system of morality, it should be open regardless of creed to all who believed that the world was supernaturally created. He set up committees which included Anglican priests, to reorganize the ritual in conformity with this view. The rituals that emerged have been practised over the intervening years to the present day, though certain grotesque penalties which had appeared in more robust times have now been removed from the Obligations. I would remind you that we are not alone in being sometimes embarrassed by an inheritance; the Church of England has a well known incumbrance of 39 articles which is still, however reluctantly, acknowledged in its liturgies. However, to return to the rituals devised by the Duke's committee, those who have used them have included members of the Royal Family, archbishops (including at least two bishops of Peterborough, Archbishop Magee and Bishop Spencer Leeson), priests of the Established Church and ministers of many other Christian denominations, which at least raises a presumption that they saw no incompatibility between Christianity and Freemasonry.

As to the basic principles of the Craft, you will see from the pamphlet[6] that they are traditionally summarized as 'brotherly love, relief and truth'. Brotherly love implies loving your neighbour, in the sense in which Christ illustrated that word in the parable of the Good

Samaritan; in the words adopted by the ritual 'doing unto him as in similar circumstances you would wish that he would do unto you.' It includes toleration towards the ideals and beliefs of others.

Coming then to 'relief', masonic charity is not limited to masonic objects only. One of our great charitable organisations, the Grand Charity, devotes a considerable part of its income to non-masonic gifts. In the year to April 1987 about £500k out of an income of some £1.5 million was spent in this way; £680k went to Masons and their dependents in need and £70k was voted to masonic charities[7]. Another charity, the Masonic Trust for Girls and Boys, looks after some 900 girls, boys and young people; their newest project is to provide hostels in inner cities so that girls coming to a strange town for vocational training or on first job can find a safe room with a warden at hand.

The needy aged are looked after by annuities, usually granted on an annual basis from the central charities, supplemented at Provincial level; and by the provision of 15 residential homes. For the sick there is the Royal Masonic Hospital where Freemasons and their dependants are admitted for treatment, paying in accordance with their means; a fund (called 'the New Samaritan Fund' and widely supported by the Lodges) tackles the resultant deficit. Non-masonic private patients are also treated there.

Away from the centre each Province is also concerned with charity, both masonic and non-masonic. The present annual income of our Provincial Benevolent fund is about £10k[8] mainly from donations by the Lodges, and Provincial Grand Lodge has authorized the expenditure of up to £1,600 a year for non-masonic purposes[9].

In the individual Lodges the Master is expected to raise money for what we call his 'list' in his year of office. This goes to the charity or charities, masonic or non-masonic, of his choice but I expect a tenth for the Provincial Benevolent Fund. Tithing again, you see; the naughty Masons imitating the Church once more.

Charity of course is not just a matter of cash. Each Lodge has an Almoner, whose duty is to see that the sick, the needy and the old are properly looked after. I try to get the Almoners in this Province to take a junior Brother with them on their rounds whenever possible; they then see the principle in practice, and those visited feel that they are being kept in touch; even the widows like to know how the Lodge is getting on. I also ask the Lodges to undertake some act of service for old people in their area.

The third great principle is Truth. Succinct, but what does it mean? Pilate had the same problem you will recall, and perhaps if he had realized his question would achieve such a world-wide circulation, particularly with Francis Bacon's comments attached, he would never have asked it. Certainly I shall not attempt an answer, but I can refer you to St Paul's Epistle to the Philippians 4:8: 'whatsoever things are honest, whatsoever things are just, whatsoever things are pure, whatsoever things are lovely, whatsoever things are of good report'. Every Freemason whether a Christian or not, would I am sure, willingly adopt that as a standard and try to attain it. The Grand Lodge leaflet, as you will have seen, links truth to morality[10].

Much more could be said but it is time to turn to the criticisms voiced in the working party's report[11]. Many are based on the faulty premise that Freemasonry is in some sense a religion. In fact it is difficult to see how a movement which requires a man to profess his religion before he is admitted and to continue to practise it after admission, can itself be termed a religion. The line between religion and morality may be finely drawn, but it is there. As to the points made about worship, of course there is worship; as Christians there is, or should be worship in every department of our lives and all we do should be done to the service of our God in accordance with the teaching of Christ and our belief in the Christian Faith. But there is a problem, and it is a problem which the report realises that the Church as well as Freemasonry must face — the validity of prayer in an inter-faith context. In the Synod the Archbishop of York, rightly in my respectful submission, took exception to the tasteless way in which the working party put the dilemma in paragraph 112[12]; but the question remains. The problem of inter-faith relationships has been outlined with perhaps rather more decorum in a booklet 'We Believe in God' prepared by the Doctrine Commission of the Church of England[13]; there, at pages 13-15 you will find a useful discussion from which the following is taken:

'. . . there is also much in Christian and other traditions which overlaps — enough to suggest that all are in touch in some degree with a single reality which, in these different idioms, is acknowledged and worshipped as God. They can become part of the resources of reason and experience which help to make explicit the doctrine of God implied in our own Scripture and tradition; and this should lead us to show openness and reverence towards the beliefs and practices of others. . . .

'We are concerned . . . with an ultimate Reality which we believe to exist , and to which we claim to have privileged access through the Scriptures and tradition preserved for us by the Church. But in seeking to go beyond the mere statement that "We believe in God", and to be more precise about what kind of a God he is, we join a conversation which has been in progress since the beginning of the

Christian religion, and which in various forms must be conducted within any "revealed religion" if that religion is to remain alive.'

For the context of that quotation I refer you to chapter 1 of the booklet but I do not think I am doing any violence to its meaning by reading only a short extract and I want to draw your attention particularly to those words; 'openness and reverence towards the beliefs and practices of others'. They seem to me to cover aptly the attitude of a Christian Freemason to Brother Masons of another faith; an attitude which has made it possible for Irish Freemasonry to be united, North and South, under one Grand Lodge; for an Arab Christian to be elected some years ago as Grand Master of the Grand Lodge of Israel; and for me to sit at lunch recently after a meeting of Supreme Grand Chapter, the governing body of the English Royal Arch Chapters, with the head of the Royal Arch in the Transvaal on one side and the head of a masonic order in Zimbabwe on the other in perfect harmony.

To return to the question of prayer, I am sure that Freemasons would strongly resist any suggestion that prayers should no longer be offered in Lodges. Nor would we wish to make it impossible for men of other faiths which require a belief in a Supreme Being to join us. If I may quote the Archbishop of York in the Synod debate, he said 'We badly need good contexts in which people with religious convictions can work together, without abandoning those convictions or without ignoring them. Freemasonry, as I understand it, has tried to provide such a context . . . I think the Craft needs to be commended for a least trying to solve an exceedingly difficult problem.' That is the end of the quotation and I leave the thought with you.

You will expect me to say something about the words on the pedestal in the Royal Arch. A lot of nonsense and some sense has been talked about these in recent months. The matter is not helped by the fact that in some Royal Arch rituals, including the one which the working party used as its basic reference, one of the words has been referred to as a name, leading to an inference that it was put forward as a name of God. This is wrong and we are concerned about it. Revision of ritual is fraught with difficulty for Freemasons, a remark which may bring a wry smile to the lips of Anglicans; but we may actually find ourselves indebted to the working party for creating a climate where we can hope to get the revision of the ritual in this and other respects through Supreme Grand Chapter in the next 12 months[14].

So, what of the future? The principles of genuine Freemasonry are simple but the Craft has been much misrepresented and much misunderstood. As a system of morality it teaches a high standard of conduct. It certainly does not teach that such conduct is the way of salvation; that would be to cross the line between morality and religion.

The Christian Freemason believes that he is saved by the sacrifice of Christ, the Redeemer and Saviour; and Freemasonry will require him to stand firm in that belief because that is the creed of his Faith. I personally have always found my Freemasonry subordinate to but supportive of my faith as a Christian and like many others I find no incompatibility between them. I am heartened by the positive attitude of the Archbishop of York and respectfully agree with him that there is a tendency to get too solemn about the matter. It is not the nicety of argument that should carry the day but the example of those Christian Freemasons who are serving their Divine Master in whatever way He may have shown them, Christians first and Freemasons second.

This debate has grieved many Freemasons, not because it is taking place, but because of the manner in which it seems to be conducted. The media have treated the report as condemnatory of Freemasonry though the working party and General Synod say it is not. The impression is harmful and hurtful, and could polarize the situation. There has been too much shouting, and it is time to talk and to listen — not only listen, but hear. The situation is not critical, but it could become so both for Freemasons and the Church, to the benefit of neither. This must not be allowed to happen. It is time to seek understanding and from understanding will come harmony.

Finally, I have tried to be constructive and to avoid emotion but I must make one personal comment before I close. I have found much happiness and companionship in Freemasonry. I have never doubted, and do not doubt, that it is consistent with my faith as a Christian; had I done so, whatever the cost I should have given it up at once.

[1] *What is Freemasonry* published by The United Grand Lodge of England, reprinted at Appendix A.

[2] See also chapters 2, 10, 14 & 15.

[3] Later figures: 1986 3,542; 1987 3,568; 1988 3,592; 1989 3,662.

[4] Later figures: 1987 136; 1988 142; 1989 146.

[5] Later figures: 1986 14,766; 1987 14,144; 1988 13,522; 1989 14,293.

[6] Appendix A. See note 1 above.

[7] For 1989 the figures were:

Relief of petitioners	£1,142,275
Other masonic charities	161,000
Non-masonic charities	1,460,150
	£2,765,425

[8] Figure for 1989 £29,940; 1990 £39,163.

[9] Figure for 1990 £3,000

[10] Appendix A. See note 1 above.

[11] *Freemasonry and Christianity* Church House Publishing: ISBN 0 7151 3716 6.

[12] Paragraph 112 of Report is reproduced at Appendix B.

[13] Church House Publishing, 19878; ISBN 0 7151 3715 8.

[14] The offending word was removed by resolution of Supreme Grand Chapter on 8 February 1989. See also chapter 12, note 3.

2

'OUR SAID MOST EXCELLENT BRETHEREN AND COMPANIONS'

How the Supreme Grand Chapter was founded and established

This book is about 'The Supreme Order of the Holy Royal Arch', recognized as part of the Craft Third Degree yet a separate Order with its own governing body and its own executive. If we are to understand this curious situation we must know why the 'Order' came into existence and how this strange unity of separation came about. The purpose of this chapter is to offer an explanation.

List of Important Dates

1717	Premier Grand Lodge founded: ('Moderns').
1753	Grand Lodge of 'the Old Institution' founded: ('Antients' or 'Atholl' Grand Lodge).
1764-66	Lord Blayney Grand Master of 'Moderns'.
1764	Caledonian Lodge obtains its 'Moderns' warrant.
1765	'The Excellent Grand and Royal Chapter' founded.
1766	June: Lord Blayney exalted.
	July: James Heseltine exalted.
	Charter of Compact Executed (22nd).
1767	Grand Secretary Spencer ('Moderns') writes letter to Frankfurt.
1784	James Heseltine, now Grand Secretary, 'Moderns', writes about the Royal Arch.
1813	The two Grand Lodges unite ('The United Grand Lodge of England').
1817	Supreme Grand Chapter formed.

THE PRELIMINARY DECLARATION in the *Book of Constitutions* of the United Grand Lodge of England states that 'By the solemn Act of Union between the two Grand Lodges of Free-Masons of England in December 1813, it was "declared and pronounced that pure Antient Masonry consists of three degrees and no more, viz., those of the Entered Apprentice, the Fellow Craft and the Master Mason, including the Supreme Order of the Holy Royal Arch" '. So too a candidate newly exalted into the Royal Arch is told that he has not thereby received a fourth degree but rather has completed his third. Yet the Order is separated from and governed independently of the Craft, an effective alliance being achieved in constitutional terms only by a minute of the United Grand Lodge to which I shall refer later, and by provisions in the Regulations of Supreme Grand Chapter requiring that every Chapter shall be attached to a regular Lodge and that certain key appointments in Grand Chapter shall be held *ex officio* by the officers holding the equivalent rank in the Craft if duly qualified. The Craft Lodge to which a Chapter is attached under Regulation 45 of the Royal Arch Regulations is responsible for its well-being and success though this is nowhere stated in the Constitutions. In theory presumably, since all the legislation rests on the regulations of Supreme Grand Chapter it could be altered by that body, and it would seem that the only retaliation available to United Grand Lodge would be to outlaw Supreme Grand Chapter. Fortunately there is no possibility of such a situation arising, though as we shall see the Royal Arch was for many years regarded as irregular by one of the two Grand Lodges which were united in 1813.

At Provincial level you can see this strange union and disunion very clearly since the Provincial Grand Master in charge of the Craft is not always also Grand Superintendent in and over the Royal Arch Province, though whenever possible the same brother will be appointed to both; and of course the appointment in the Craft is made by the Most Worshipful The Grand Master while that in the Chapter is made by the Most Excellent First Grand Principal, the same person 'if duly qualified'. When the two appointments in a Province are held by separate individuals each of them is in theory independent of the other except in certain cases; for instance, a member suspended by the head of one of the two Orders is automatically suspended in the other. Yet the good of Freemasonry demands that the two work closely together, and in the rare cases when that has not happened such is the need for practical unity that seldom, to put it mildly, has the Province achieved its full potential.

This phenomenon of unity with separation has consequences which the Royal Arch Mason must understand if he is to explain the relevance of the Chapter to a brother who has not yet been exalted into it[1]. The reasons are historical as we shall see; for the chapter heading, 'Our said Most Excellent Bretheren and Companions' is a quotation from the Charter of Compact which established the first Grand Chapter in the world, the direct ancestor of our own Supreme Grand Chapter. It was set up by the authority of Lord Blayney, Grand Master of the Premier Grand Lodge of England (one of those united in 1813), purporting to act as such in spite of the fact that his Grand Lodge had not authorized him to do so and officially considered the Royal Arch to be an undesirable innovation[2].

Before considering the historical reasons for this division it is appropriate to ask whether it has had any practical consequences. Unhesitatingly my answer is that it has, because while this strange relationship may have built a bridge it has also constructed a barrier, and that barrier hinders the completion by the Freemason of his progress to a full understanding of 'pure Antient Masonry'. So we as Royal Arch Companions must recognize that the barrier exists, understand how it arose, and be able to guide our brethren in the Craft across the bridge to become our Companions.

Every Freemason thinks of his progress from Entered Apprentice to Fellowcraft and thence to Master Mason as natural and inevitable; but although the Royal Arch is recognized as completing and being part of the Third Degree, in practice it is not always treated as such even by Lodges which are responsible for a Chapter. As a separate Order, with distinct regalia, a totally different arrangement of the Lodge room, and having as officers brethren other than those of the Lodge to which it is attached and often of considerable seniority in the Craft, as well as other differences, the Royal Arch in fact gives brethren who are not yet members of the Order the strong impression that it is something quite distinct from the Craft. It can therefore appear as no more related to the Craft than to other Orders in the Hiramic tradition such as Mark and Cryptic (Royal and Select) Masonry each of which is considered in some Constitutions to be part of ancient Freemasonry. That sense of separation is a psychological factor which we as Royal Arch Masons must actively help our brethren to overcome. We are helped in this by the fact that the Master Mason's degree is so obviously unfinished in its outcome, and the Craft teaching while admirable and practical in itself is so obviously concerned mainly with our earthbound existence, that anyone who thinks seriously about his Freemasonry must feel that it leaves him with an uncompleted story on the one hand and with a philosophy that has been only partially developed on the other. We all know that we are mortal, that we must eventually die — and to quote familiar words from the Bible which are also used in the ritual of another Order, 'the wisest of us knoweth not how soon'. We have all professed in Open Lodge our belief in a Supreme Being; we must believe that our lives should have meaning and purpose in a greater context than the purely material; and so it is natural to feel, as we think about the Craft degrees through which we have passed, that those elements of meaning and purpose are left unresolved and that the high intent and design indicated at our Initiation into Freemasonry and implicit in the questions we then answered have somehow been lost in a maze of ritual words and movements. It is left to the Royal Arch to guide us towards considering all this in the context of eternity and the duty to God enjoined by religion.

This does not imply that the Royal Arch is itself more than a code of morality. Freemasonry is in no sense a religion and though the Order may and should lead us to think about religion it does not try to provide a substitute. In 1962 United Grand Lodge affirmed this in the following words, recently confirmed as representing our attitude on this most important point:

'It cannot be too strongly asserted that Masonry is neither a religion nor a substitute for religion. Masonry seeks to inculate in its members a standard of conduct and behaviour which it believes to be acceptable to all creeds, but studiously refrains from intervening in the field of dogma or theology. Masonry therefore, is not a competitor with religion though in the the sphere of human conduct it may be hoped that its teaching will be complementary to that of religion. On the other hand its basic requirement that every member of the Order shall believe in a Supreme Being and the stress laid upon his duty towards Him should be sufficient evidence to all but the wilfully prejudiced that Masonry is an upholder of religion since it both requires a man to have some form of religious belief before he can be admitted as a Mason, and expects him when admitted to go on practising his religion.'

You may think that I am placing more stress on philosophical matters than the average Freemason is willing to bear. But again and again I am made aware how earnestly people of all conditions are searching today to bring meaning and purpose into their lives. The support the British formerly derived from self-confidence, and indeed self-importance, seems largely to have disappeared today and in its passing has left a gap in which many flounder. Some men come into Freemasonry from curiosity, but many, many more come because they are seeking for something that supports high standards of conduct and morality in this troubled and uncertain world, as well as for the fellowship of others who are at once good companions and inspired by the wish to do something constructive with their lives; the recent campaign of slander against the Craft has made no difference to this, mainly I think because on a person to person basis every Freemason is an ambassador for the whole movement and most reasonable people will judge us as they find us. This is a good reason for being open about your membership of the Craft.

It is for all these reasons, as well as the unsatisfying end of the Third Degree, that I believe a brother should be encouraged to come into the Chapter as soon as it is clear that he is ready to benefit from its teaching and companionship; and of course as soon as he is in he should be encouraged and helped by being asked to join in the work. I deplore the ideas that a brother should not be exalted until he is in office in his Lodge and that the work should only be undertaken by the officers of the Chapter. Each of these fallacies — as I consider them to be — can mean that a brother's full masonic potential is not realized and, more importantly, that his unspoken anxieties are unresolved and his unvoiced questions are left unanswered. For these reasons, among others, I wholeheartedly support the use of the catachetical method of giving the lectures; it involves junior Companions and Past Principals in the work of the Chapter and it encourages and stimulates the interest of the juniors in endeavouring to master the lessons the Order is trying to teach. To be a man's Companion means and demands much more than to be his Brother.

Now it is time to return to the earlier point, that we cannot appreciate the strange position of Royal Arch Masonry in relation to the Craft without a knowledge of the historical background, the most important factor in which is the great quarrel between the two rival Grand Lodges in London, that of the so-called 'Moderns' who were of course the original or Premier Grand Lodge, and that of their rivals, the self-styled 'Antients'.

The Premier Grand Lodge had been founded in 1717 by the four 'time immemorial' Lodges of which three still survive. It was the first ever to be founded in speculative Freemasonry as we know it and though at the start of its career it may not have aimed so high, it eventually claimed jurisdiction over all English Lodges. This claim was not at first widely accepted and indeed eight years later an old Lodge in York set up the imposingly styled 'Grand Lodge of ALL England' which later constituted half of the Lodge of Antiquity, one of the 'time immemorial' founders of the Premier Grand Lodge, into 'The Grand Lodge of England South of the River Trent' — but that story of masonic infighting is another matter. The serious challenge to the claims of the Premier Grand Lodge to pre-eminence arose from the foundation in London of 'The Most Ancient and Honourable Society of Free and Accepted Masons' whose Grand Lodge is generally held to have come into existence in 1751. Its members accused the Premier Grand Lodge of violating the ancient landmarks of the Order. There may well have been some justice in this claim if in fact, as was alleged, it had altered the modes of recognition; but it had also annoyed both Scottish and Irish Freemasons, of whom there seem to have been a considerable number in London at that time, and it may well be that they had a hand in fomenting the discontent. It was at one time believed that the founders of this new Grand Lodge, which acquired or adopted the nickname of 'Antients' and dubbed its rivals the 'Moderns', were rebels from the Premier Grand Lodge but Brother Henry Sadler, a former Grand Librarian of the United Grand Lodge, has shown that this is untrue[3].

As a result of this Freemasonry in England was split into two warring camps for the rest of the century. Consequently English Freemasons were too involved in their own quarrels, and later in trying to reconcile the two Grand Lodges, to have time to pay much attention to the explosive activities in regard to the establishment of new 'masonic' degrees taking place elsewhere, notably in France, Prussia, the West Indies and on the North American continent. Freemasonry had been exported to those territories and avidly developed to such an extent that over 1,000 so-called masonic degrees have been counted.

However, the Royal Arch did become heavily involved in the quarrel. It was becoming known here at the time when the new Grand Lodge was formed though it does not seem to have been adopted by then as a regular masonic degree by many English Lodges. It is not necessary here to discuss the vexed questions of how it originated, or how it came to have the form in which it is practised here today; but in the mid-18th century it was considered by some to be a degree of immemorial tradition while others regarded it as an unacceptable innovation and anathema. When in 1751 the 'Antients' established their Grand Lodge which claimed to be devoted to expunging innovations from the system, they were already showing their partiality and support for the Royal Arch; and they lost no time in peddling their wares, claiming to be the 'Grand Lodge of the Four Degrees' and so by implication deriding the Premier Grand Lodge as presiding only over three. They pressed the claims of the degree with vigour, to such an extent that their second Grand Secretary, the famous Laurence Dermott, called it 'the root, heart and marrow of Freemasonry'.

The Premier Grand Lodge, the 'Moderns', having been again upstaged, now set its face resolutely against the Royal Arch and in 1759 in a letter which its Grand Secretary wrote to an Irish Freemason, these words occur: 'Our Society is neither Arch, Royal Arch or

Antient, so that you have no right to partake of our Charity' — chilling words which Dermott promptly incorporated into his own Grand Lodge's propaganda. That was, and for a long time remained, the official 'Moderns' view even though many of their Grand Officers seem to have been exalted into the Order including, as we shall see, their own Grand Master in 1766; yet in 1767 the Grand Secretary of the 'Moderns' wrote officially to a brother in Frankfurt that 'the Royal Arch is a society which we do not acknowledge and which we hold to be an invention to introduce innovation and to seduce the Brethren'; it had certainly seduced his Grand Master.

In such a topsy-turvy world, who better to find a solution than an Irishman? Cadwallader, ninth Lord Blayney, became Grand Master of the premier Grand Lodge in 1764. In the same year Caledonian Lodge in London seceded from the 'Antients' under whose banner had been constituted only shortly before, and joined the 'Moderns' as number 325; its present number is 134. In 1765, apparently with the help of that Lodge, 29 'Modern' Freemasons brought a new Royal Arch Chapter into being; it was called 'The Excellent Grand and Royal Chapter', a grandiose name which suggests that from its inception it was intended for a special role. That this role may well have been the founding of a Grand Chapter is supported by the fact that even today in warrants and patents sealed by Supreme Grand Chapter the attestation clause still refers to 'Our Excellent Grand and Royal Chapter'.

In 1766 Lord Blayney was exalted into this Chapter; he was still Grand Master of the Premier Grand Lodge which had not been consulted in the matter and certainly would not recognize the right of the 29 brethren, even with the support and approval of the Grand Master, to establish a governing body for a degree which they officially considered not to be within their system of Freemasonry; nor could those brethren claim that their conduct was in any way regular, in view of the official attitude. Yet Blayney was to claim, as we shall see, that he acted under his powers as Grand Master.

On exaltation Blayney seems to have become automatically and forthwith First Principal of the Chapter and to have taken the title 'Head of the Royal Arch' — rapid promotion indeed. At the next meeting of the Chapter, in July, James Heseltine, Grand Steward in the 'Moderns' Grand Lodge, was exalted.

Bearing in mind that the Frankfurt letter already quoted was written in the year after Lord Blayney's exaltation, it is clear that by now there was considerable schizophrenia among the 'Moderns' in regard to the Royal Arch; indeed this persisted for some time since eight years later James Heseltine, by now their Grand Secretary and yet not only a member of the Excellent Grand and Royal Chapter but also one of those who had signed the Charter by which as we shall see the Grand Chapter was established, had to write officially to a foreign correspondent in these terms:

> 'It is true that many of the Fraternity belong to a degree in Masonry which is said to be higher than the other, and is called Royal Arch. I have the honour to belong to this degree . . . but it is not acknowledged in Grand Lodge, and all its emblems and jewels are forbidden to be worn there . . . You will see that the Royal Arch is a private and distinct society. It is part of Masonry, but has no connection with Grand Lodge.'

From this letter it is clear that at least some 'Moderns' were admitting that the Royal Arch was a masonic degree or order, so perhaps some progress had been made; but the claim that it 'has no connection with Grand Lodge' clearly implies that Lord Blayney's action was unconstitutional and, as we shall see, there is some evidence that this is how it was regarded in some official quarters. However, Grand Lodge and the Grand and Royal Chapter continued in a state of wary co-existence until the time when negotiations for the union of the two Grand Lodges were nearing the fruition achieved in 1813.

The Excellent Grand and Royal Chapter with Lord Blayney at its head and many influential 'Moderns' as members was very active in 1766. Blayney had been exalted in June and in July it met three times; at each meeting he presided. At the first it was agreed that a document, to be called 'Charter of Compact' should be prepared which would in effect set up a Grand Chapter. The fact that it was to be called a charter is interesting because documents of constitution issued by Grand Lodges were generally known as charters or warrants, so the name would smack of authority in the masonic world and would certainly suggest that Blayney was acting by virtue of his position and the authority it implied. It was executed on 22 July. In it Blayney, describing himself as 'Grand Master of Free and Accepted Masons, and also Most Excellent Grand Master of the Royal Arch of Jerusalem . . . having duly passed the Royal Arch', declared 'for the Honour, Dignity, Preservation and Welfare of the Royal Craft' (rather strange words when his Grand Lodge had not sanctioned what was being done and did not officially recognize the Degree the new body was to govern), 'We do by these presents as much as in us lyes' — belated caution here perhaps? — 'Institute, and Erect our said Most Excellent Bretheren and Companions . . . and their Successors . . . jointly with Ourselves and Our Successors Most Excellent Grand Master for the time being from Time to Time and at all Times hereafter to form and be The Grand and Royal Chapter of the Royal Arch of Jerusalem . . .'. It is worth noting that at some later time the date on the Charter was altered to make it appear that it had been executed in 1767 when Blayney's term of office as Grand Master had expired, and the letter 'P' for 'Past' was skillfully inserted before the words 'Grand Master'. Perhaps this was an attempt to suggest that the Premier Grand Lodge had nothing to do with it (which would be strictly correct) or that its execution was *ultra vires*; or perhaps it was to ward off an attack on the new body as irregular and unauthorized. But whatever the legal position, the Grand Chapter was there to stay.

For once the initiative had passed to the 'Moderns' and the 'Antients' were unable to react effectively because they had already made great capital out of their claim to be 'the Grand Lodge of the Four Degrees'. They did rally sufficiently five years later in 1771 to create their own Grand Chapter but it never seems to have become more than a committee or at best only a pale shadow of their Grand Lodge; certainly it was never a truly independent masonic authority — a fact that was to cause problems later.

The story now moves on to the 19th century and the end of the division between the two Grand Lodges. In 1813, after much preparation, HRH the Duke of Sussex as Grand Master of the Premier Grand Lodge and his brother HRH the Duke of Kent as Grand Master of the rival Grand Lodge presided over the union of the two to form the United Grand Lodge of Ancient Freemasons of England. Rather more than a year before that the Duke of Sussex as First Grand Principal, reporting in The Grand and Royal Chapter on the negotiations for union, stated that four degrees were to be acknowledged; and just before the actual union he was invested by that body 'with the fullest powers to negotiate a union of the Grand Lodges' in such a manner as might appear to be 'most conducive to the general interests of Masonry'. It may seem odd that Grand Chapter should purport to grant authority to negotiate a union of the Grand Lodges (who had in any case substantially agreed the terms of union between themselves) but we must remember that though for the 'Antients' the Royal Arch was part of the Craft the 'Moderns' Grand Lodge could not speak for it as they did not, at least officially, recognize The Grand and Royal Chapter or the Order over which it presided as part of their system.

Not surprisingly responsibility for government of the Royal Arch after the union was far from clear and there is evidence of confusion. The Act of Union had specifically accepted that the Order was genuinely part of Freemasonry; but its actual status had not been defined further and though the Excellent Grand and Royal Chapter still existed in theory (and indeed in law), the so-called Grand Chapter of the Antients, having been a mere committee of their Grand Lodge, had presumably ceased to exist at the Union. It was not until March 1817, three and a quarter years after the union, that a ceremony was devised to give at least a semblance of order to a disordered situation. Members of the Excellent Grand and Royal Chapter and former members of the Antients 'Grand Chapter' met in separate rooms and opened Chapters before proceeding into a third room where the Duke of Sussex received them and formally joined them as one. Six months later United Grand Lodge at a Quarterly Communication noted what it called the 'junction' of 'the two Grand Chapters' and — here we come to the minute referred to earlier — 'Resolved unanimously That the Grand Lodge will at all times be disposed to acknowledge the proceedings of the Grand Chapter, and, so long as their arrangements do not interfere with the Regulations of the Grand Lodge, and are in conformity with the Act of Union, they will be ready to recognize, facilitate, and uphold the same'. The cautious wording suggests that United Grand Lodge realised that the Royal Arch had acquired a separate status and was in theory at least wholly independent, and indeed that neither it nor its predecessors had been parties to the Act of Union. But the body which we now call Supreme Grand Chapter had been formally established and its control of the Order it represents had been recognized. However, it was not until 1834 that formal steps to unify and 'universalise'[4] the ritual began.

The last step in the story took place in 1853 when the Preamble to the Craft Constitutions took its present form, which follows the wording of the Act of Union.

Earlier in this chapter it was stated that we must understand both the barrier and the bridge between Craft and Royal Arch. We have seen that the reasons for the separation of the two Orders are basically historical; but the reasons for sympathy between them are strong indeed and historical accident should not prevent us from seeing and understanding the full pattern of 'pure Antient Masonry' — the pattern of an incomplete Third Degree which can only be made complete by exaltation. The Royal Arch does not merely perfect the Master Mason's education in masonic history and secrets; in a phrase I have often used, it places Freemasonry in the context of eternity. It is to be taken seriously and not every Master Mason will be ready for its teaching as soon as he has been raised; but *properly presented* (and those words need to be stressed) it has much to offer to the world in which we live, uncertain of its values but seeking earnestly for truth in a civilisation threatened as never before. We fail in our duty to our brethren if we do not realize the importance of this Order today and study it so that we can with sincerity and conviction encourage

Master Masons to join us in it. As they realize that the Craft teaching and legend leaves them with an earthbound system of morality and finally with a tale of loss, death and despair, they will see that there must be more and any Companion of this Order must be able to explain to them that the Royal Arch looks further, that its legend is one of discovery and that its message is that we live in the light and glory of eternity.

Your first practical step in this is the simple one of remembering to wear your Royal Arch breast jewel on all Craft occasions and to encourage questions about it; equip yourself to answer those questions by thinking out what Royal Arch Masonry means to you, not just in theory but in practice. Above all remember that this is a companionable Order and while regarding and respecting its serious side we should also enjoy our meetings, both in Chapter and at refreshment; to do so is in the true Royal Arch tradition, for its is recorded that in the very early days of Grand Chapter the annual festival was followed by a ball and supper to which Master Masons and their ladies were invited. The minutes record that after an elegant supper, the evening concluded with that Harmony and Social Mirth which has ever been the peculiar criterion of Masons and true Citizens of the World. The factors that will attract Master Masons to become Companions are neither duty nor idle curiosity, but the knowledge that the teaching of the Order is serious and meaningful, coupled with an awareness that we are happy in it and enjoy that real and meaningful companionship which must at all times be the hallmark of the Order and which explains why each of us is so proud and so content to be called by the title of 'Companion.

---

[1] In a Lodge which gives *Peterborough Booklet No 3* to the newly-raised brother, he will have read about the Holy Royal Arch in pages 7-8 ('THE NEXT STEP'). The booklets are published and distributed by QCCC Ltd, 60 Great Queen Street, London WC2B 5BA.

[2] See 'Frankfurt' letter referred to later in this chapter.

[3] *Masonic Facts and Fictions* by Henry Sadler, 1887. Reprinted 1985, Aquarian Press, ISBN 0 85030 440 7.

[4] In current masonic use the regrettable term 'universalise' signifies the removal from rituals of references to specific religions.

3
THE CANDIDATE (1978)

The fact that every year at the annual meeting of Provincial Grand Chapter a Grand Superintendent is expected to address the Companions provides an opportunity to express thanks for all that has been done in the past 12 months and good wishes for the year ahead as well as to offer comment and advice. When, in 1978, I was put in charge of the Province of Northamptonshire and Huntingdonshire as Grand Superintendent the Installation took place at the annual Convocation and there was little opportunity to do more than express thanks to the team who came from London to conduct the ceremony and those who had worked so hard to make the occasion a success, and to welcome our many visitors. But there was time to say something about the treatment of candidates and an updated version of that part of the Address is reproduced here.

THERE IS NO need to tell you, Companions, that we depend on the Craft for the flow of candidates to our Order, as indeed does every other masonic Order practised in the Province. But it is important that we should give thought to how we can attract them, and once they have been exalted, how we can retain their interest and inspire them to wish to take office and to begin to play their part in the Chapter. In this the first essential is that you should yourselves have thought about the Order and be able to explain what is its attraction for you.

Too often candidates are recruited rather than attracted, and recruited for the wrong reason, for instance because otherwise there would be no ceremony, or because a senior brother says something like 'It's high time you were in the Chapter'. But you can only attract a man into Chapter if you can explain why you are yourself attracted by the Order. To be able to do that may demand some thought on your part but it will be something you will find well worth while.

What then do you explain to a possible candidate? For a start you can tell him that it is recognized as the completion of the Third Degree, as a glance at the Preamble to the Craft Constitutions will show. It is a good thing to point out this soon after he has been raised, and the presentation of his Grand Lodge Certificate provides a perfect opportunity. If you are asked to explain what you mean by 'completing the Third Degree' you can remind him that the legend of that degree ended in loss, despair and death and tell him that the Royal Arch is concerned with finding what was lost and has a message of hope[1]. But even then he will only want to join if he sees that you really enjoy the Chapter, as you will if you do your part to see that the meetings are happy and enjoyable — and that includes making sure that you understand the ritual and do not merely learn it parrot-fashion.

The need to look after a candidate does not stop when he has been exalted. Unless he has been absorbed into the companionship of the Chapter he is unlikely to be sufficiently appreciative to be able to understand its value, and he will get bored and stop attending. That is the worst disaster that can befall a Chapter and is a potent criticism of its members. Even if there is no exaltation ceremony in prospect there is plenty of other work available at the expense of a little effort — lectures, explanations of the banners, the whole symbolism of the Order; and the 'new boy' can and should be invited to take part; and if a Past Principal is appointed to help him and to prompt, you have involved two Companions in one piece of work. Then, when he has done his part, there is the duty of thanking him, congratulating him on achievement and affording kindly guidance if anything went wrong. All this is part of turning a brotherhood into a companionship.

[1] The Peterborough booklet *Why Join the Royal Arch* may help.

4
THE SUPREME ORDER (1979)

The full title of the Order as stated in the Preamble to the Constitutions of the United Grand Lodge of England (quoting form the Act of Union between the two London Grand Lodges in 1813) is 'The Supreme Order of the Holy Royal Arch'. A good starting point for any attempt to understand it would be to investigate the claims implicit in that title. Half of the 1979 Address was devoted to this. It was the response to this which finally persuaded me to continue in this vein, and the subsequent Addresses were therefore devoted entirely to seeking to discover what messages the Order held for us in today's world. It was to prove a demanding but fascinating task the reward of which was the interest that was inspired.

OUR ANNUAL CONVOCATION is a time when we can look forward and backward with profit and provides a good opportunity for stocktaking. So on this occasion I would ask you to think for a moment about the name of this Order, 'the Supreme Order of the Holy Royal Arch' and to ask yourself how we can justify so startling a title? For if you think of what that title implies you may well find that you are somewhat startled at its import. We are so used to the words that familiarity allows us to gloss over the magnitude of their meaning. But do you not think that we, who call ourselves not merely members of, but Companions in an Order bearing so resounding a title should give some thought to how that that title is justified?

One argument that will be put forward of course is that this is mere high flown language or hyperbole since a claim to be superior is one of the well known steps in the process of convincing oneself and others of one's own superiority. I believe that historical analysis of the Order as we now know it shows this argument to be false. The brethren who naturally and rightly wished to know and be admitted to the genuine secrets at which the Third Degree hints, were asking to be taught the answer to a question posed but not answered by that Degree; posed that is by the ritual itself. They hoped to know more, whatever their motives. Quite possibly they did not feel superior; but how much more must they have been influenced by the very human need for completeness in knowledge? No doubt references to 'inevitable destiny' and 'peace and salvation' were not explicit enough for them. But what stands out, indeed shines out, from those early days is the fact that they found not just knowledge but understanding, for they had to face the supreme riddle — the relationship between man and his Creator. Intimations of immortality had replaced the emblems of mortality. Does more need to be said to justify the title 'Supreme Order'? Surely not.

So what of 'the Holy Royal Arch'? Of the Arch we all know; the strongest bond in masonry, that which in speculative Freemasonry welds Brethren into Companions. It is 'royal' because it looks to the legendary royal Grand Masters who built the first Temple. It is 'holy'. a word not to be used lightly, because the arch of the vault concealed the altar upon which the Ineffable Name had been placed, the altar which we commemorate in every Royal Arch Chapter by the pedestal which stands in our midst at every meeting and which your Grand Chapter certificate places on the chequered pavement of mortal joy and sorrow, but which yet draws the eye to the shining star of eternity.

For that is what this Order is about. It puts Craft Freemasonry into the framework of eternity. It demands a sense of wonder and commitment; and it gives us to build upon, one of the loveliest visions a candidate for any masonic degree ever sees. You, as members of Provincial Grand Chapter, have a duty to see that the impetus, the awareness of that moment is nurtured and grows. This means striving for proficiency in the work since that is a necessary qualification if the ritual is to be readily understood. If you are responsible for allotting work it means also that you must help those to whom you give it, 'supply their defects' as the Address to the Principals rather charmingly puts it[1]; and you must see that as many Companions take part as is reasonably possible, since this is not merely more interesting for the Chapter but more useful by way of instruction for the Companions who are involved. Above all, you must see that your Chapter ceremonies are stimulating. What is important is not that one Companion should be the acknowledged expert on one part of the ritual but that as many Companions as possible should study and understand it, and that it be performed for the benefit of the Chapter rather than for the gratification of the performer. The lessons will only be learnt if the work in Chapter is both enjoyable and enjoyed; and Freemasonry is something to be enjoyed.

[1] From the *Perfect Ceremonies* Royal Arch Ritual.

5
THE SOJOURNERS' STORY (1980)

The Sojourners' story is one of real drama, so much so perhaps that we concentrate on the narrative and forget that it is also full of allegory. Any search for the lessons taught by the Order will naturally look to it at an early stage; so it came next in the search.

The Royal Arch is often said to complete the Third Degree because it concerns the finding of that which was lost. This never seemed wholly satisfactory, and yet there was something incomplete about that Degree. When some years later the Royal Arch ritual was revised by the deletion of the recognition word, the 'loss' theme became even more difficult to understand. Over the years I have come to the conclusion that while it is correct to say that the Royal Arch does complete the teaching of the Craft it is not so much by finding something physically lost as by supplying what was missing, the sense of an all-pervading eternity in which our lives are set. Nevertheless, there was something found by the Sojourners; and it was only later that I saw what should have been obvious from the start, that the discovery came about because the God of Israel had spoken to a Persian monarch — a heathen.

The Jews had not regularly and faithfully kept up the worship of the God Who had brought them out of Egypt, and after the building of Solomon's Temple there were times when even the Sacred Scroll of the Law was lost: see for instance the episode recorded in 2 Kings, 22.8, where the story is told of the religious revival that followed its discovery in the reign of Josiah less than 40 years before the destruction of the Temple by Nebuchadnezzar. So there was a real symbolism in the discovery of the Scroll and of the Ineffable Name; God did keep faith and might even reveal His will through the medium of those not of the Jewish race. But in 1980 this realisation lay in the future[1].

This was the first occasion on which the Address was wholly given over to a consideration of the esoteric meaning of the Order. Some of the thoughts in it are developed further in Chapter 16, 'From Babylon, Most Excellent'.

24

WITH THE INVESTITURE of the new officers we begin to look forward to the session which is now starting, when we shall again pass on to those who in course of time will succeed us the story that had been handed down to us — a tale full of wonder, one that we hear so often that we may be in danger of forgetting its magic and its mystery. To me, it is still full of unsuspected meaning; there is continually something new to be learnt from it.

Think for a moment about the central part of the story. Three men returned from captivity in a foreign land where on at least one occasion they had been in danger of wholesale massacre because they were Jews[2]. They came back to the ruins of the city of their great king, David; the city in which his son, Solomon, under whom their nation had seen its greatest age, had built a House dedicated to their God, the House where the Ark which bore witness to the covenant of God with His people had finally come to rest. To them the city was sacred, part of their history, made more precious because until then they knew it only by repute; now they saw it, the destined place where God Who had long before brought their race out of captivity in Egypt, and Who now brought their generation out of Babylon had decreed He would cause His Sacred Name to dwell. They came to a city; they found a desolation, a deserted ruin. Where once the Temple had proclaimed the majesty of God and the authority of His people all that was most sacred to them lay forlorn and ravaged. It must have been a vivid reminder of the disobedience which had led them into captivity. Small wonder that they were content to be employed in a menial task so long as it related to the rebuilding of the House.

There then they toiled, dutifully clearing away the rubble and the ruin, until one day they came upon carving of such beauty that they paused and probed it with great care, finding first one, then another pillar 'of exquisite beauty and symmetry' and a way between them. Now they began to order their work to follow the line of the path they had found. It guided them past six more pairs of pillars; did they realise that they were being led below the place where the Holy of Holies had stood? And then — nothing. Only solid rock. In disappointment and frustration one of them struck the ground with his crowbar and it met the earth with a hollow sound. They looked again and found that they were standing on masonry. They opened the vault and the long lost treasures were found.

Do you notice once again here that constant contrast between the Craft and the Royal Arch, the contrast of the ephemeral and the eternal? When the ground was opened by the trusty Fellow-Crafts in the Craft legend, they found a mortal body; when the Sojourners opened the vault an altar to God was revealed.

The chamber in which the secrets had lain hidden for some 500 years was apparently plain, but its furnishings if simple were magnificent; an altar of virgin marble surmounted by a plate of gold hidden beneath a veil placed there by — well, by whom? One of the fabled Grand Masters? King Solomon himself? Who could tell? Who can tell now? It matters not. What does matter is that for all those years it could have lain there, its very existence unsuspected, awaiting that moment.

For think back now over those 500 years to the days when we are told that the vault was first built and the secret passage constructed. Very few could have known of it. What the world would see and was meant to see was the splendour of the Temple which the king, following the command of God, had built to house the Ark and Mercy Seat under the great outspread wings of the cherubim; the building whose costliness and splendour had been the object of admiration to the surrounding nations and whose fame had spread to the then known world. It was there in Jerusalem for anyone to see and admire. Resplendent in gold, furnished with wealth and splendour, the sacred shrine of the Jewish people at the height of their power, it was calculated to impress and to compel an envious admiration. To the Israelites at large and to the outside world, that was surely what the Temple meant. It inspired, it was meant to inspire, the awe and wonder which vividly mirrored the power and the glory of God, and to convince all other peoples of inferiority.

Yet all the time, unseen and unsuspected, below the most sacred part of that Temple the Royal Arch legend says that there reposed an inner secret which was to outlast the splendour; in an underground vault, without show or ostentation, the Grand Masters had placed the Ineffable Name with the sacred scrolls and vouched their authenticity by causing their own names to be inscribed there.

It does not matter how time may have distorted the legend over the intervening centuries. What does matter, or rather one of the many things that matter, is that we should realize the contrast between the outward appearance and the hidden heart. There was no inconsistency. The Temple proclaimed to all the power and majesty of God; the secrets were for those chosen to share them. All could see the Temple; only the initiated knew what it concealed.

So it should be with Freemasonry. In this sense are we charged to practise out of the Lodge those duties we have been taught in it; in this sense are we instructed to prove to the world what manner of men Freemasons are so that even those who are not of our fraternity may understand that at our hands they may expect compassion, sympathy, justice and charity, and may know that, though we do not as

Freemasons proselytize for any one religion, we revere the Creator and each of us practises whatever religion he professes.

Let me quote from the final paragraph of an Address given in 1985 by RW Bro E. L. Baillieu in his capacity at that time of Assistant Grand Master of the United Grand Lodge of England; speaking at a masonic meeting in Australia he said 'The world regards us as a secret society essentially concerned with the welfare of Masons and their dependents, and possessing very few principles. Young men ought to be clamouring to join us, but they are not doing so, not because they cannot afford to, but because they are given no sufficient indication of what we stand for — our system of morality and our concern for the whole human species. I am convinced that Masonry requires from us a positive and not a passive role. To be worthy of our principles we must do something in the short span allowed us to improve the society in which we live; we cannot properly sit back and leave the task to others.'

We must of course, as in effect Bro Baillieu went on to say, be jealous of our secrets; but that does not mean we must hold our Freemasonry so secluded and so wrapped in mystery that the world in its ignorance is left to think of us as selfish, self-centred and uncaring. Where the dividing line between secrecy and concealment lies in something each of us has to decide for himself. All I ask is that you consider it and make your own decision, and that you do not unduly criticize those who may, as they will, put the dividing line a little further one way or the other than you yourself may have placed it.

Above all, Companions, do not become so circumspect or constrained that it in any way inhibits your own enjoyment with your brethren. Freemasonry should be enjoyed; our meetings should be happy and companionable occasions. Much of our strength lies in the way in which solemnity of procedure and cheerful companionship are mingled in all our meetings, both in and out of the Lodge room; and in that and in the face we openly present to the world will lie our future. Each of us has his part to play in ensuring that our Fraternity develops and advances for the benefit of mankind in general as much as for that of Freemasonry in particular. So, Companions, keep the secret vault secure but do not be afraid to let the world glimpse the glories of the Temple.

1 See Chapter 13.
2 See the story of Haman, Mordeccai and Queen Esther in the *Apocrypha* (Book of Esther, Chapters 13-16).

6
A MOMENT TO REMEMBER (1981)

It has been said that every Masonic Order has its magic moment. The Royal Arch is no exception but though the candidate is left feeling that something special has happened, nowhere in the ritual is he helped to discover what that moment means or why it is special. It is embedded in the ritual as a tableau but even those who take part have rarely given thought to what it is that they are portraying; consequently they have no incentive to do their part in making it meaningful. In Chapters in which every Companion is involved at this point, the ceremony is much enhanced by their participation; but even in those in which the only members to move are the three Principals the meaning is there. In this Address the working adopted in my own Province is of course reflected; it is that used in many others and while it would be presumptuous to suggest that it is more than just one way of portrayal, it is to many the most satisfying in this respect.

WE ARE TAUGHT that Freemasonry is a system of morality, veiled in allegory and illustrated by symbols. The morality and the code of conduct that it implies are taught by ritual and the ritual has to be learnt. This demands a concentration and effort which is, and indeed must be seriously undertaken and that necessity does conceal a danger, the danger that the compulsion to learn and the fear of failing may rob the words of meaning. So too if the ceremonial of the Order is carried out merely as an exercise in following the rubric or appeasing a Director of Ceremonies the effect will be lost, as it will be if it is not undertaken for the benefit of the candidate, if the words are not spoken to him, or the requirements of the rubric are not carried out with him in mind. Never consider yourself as you take part in our ceremonies; think always about the candidate. You will not only make the ceremony of exaltation more intelligible for him and his reception more enjoyable but you will find that you help the rest of the companions and yourself in doing so. Ritual and ceremonial are a means to an end; when either becomes an end in itself, it is a dead end.

When you have work to do in the Royal Arch, try always to think of its meaning and effect; you will find that in doing so you learn much more than the ritual, and there is so much more to be learnt. Last year I suggested to you a parallel between the universally visible Temple and the concealed vault on the one hand, and our public attitude to our Freemasonry on the other. That was one example; let me direct your attention to another.

A candidate stands at the door of the Chapter. He has been examined in the three Craft degrees and has been entrusted in reliance on his Craft Obligations. It is almost certain that he is already well acquainted with the Companion who has carried out these duties, and quite likely that he has seen, or seen a picture of, a Lodge room set out for a Chapter meeting. He will not have the apprehensions that may beset an Initiate in the Craft and will know that no harmful or untoward thing will confront him. He probably has a mild curiosity as to what lies ahead but there is no question of a wild rush forward or an endeavour to retreat; there is no likelihood that he will refuse to take an Obligation — he has already taken at least three and well understands the nature of a masonic promise. So, why is he blindfolded?

The ritual gives an an answer of sorts. Man would have remained in the darkness of ignorance and error but for Divine revelation. An allegory, yes; but this has never seemed to me enough to justify that blindfold. However, there is something else, something of the greatest importance which depends entirely on his inability to see before the right and effective moment. As with so many of our really profound masonic mysteries it is something not at once apparent and the significance of which only emerges later as one advances step by step through this mortal life. It happens in one quick moment, without explanation, and then it has gone; but I do not think it is ever forgotten. It begins in the instant that the blindfold is removed and it ends as the candidate turns away to retire.

When he is restored to light in the Royal Arch the new Companion sees before him a carefully contrived tableau. He will appreciate it as such but whether he ever fully appreciates its meaning will depend on whether it has been thoughtfully and carefully undertaken by his Companions. Let us look with the light of knowledge at what he sees and think of what it portrays.

In front of him is the broken arch, the symbol of the effort he has made to find the way of truth, which indeed he cannot find without a conscious act of will and the teaching of his religion, as well as toil of mind and body. Beyond the Arch lies the floorcloth with the chequered pattern which represents our journey through this mortal life with its alternating pattern of joy and sorrow. Ahead, towards the

East, there rests on the chequered cloth a pedestal with a veil which, as he will soon learn, conceals the Ineffable Name and which can only be reached, and the true teaching of the Order understood, by treading the way before him and deviating neither to right nor to left. On his journey he will have to grapple with the forces of nature, represented by the Platonic bodies; and the tools which lie before him give a warning that further work and effort will be needed to reach the goal, while the trowel and sword remind him to build soundly and be ready to defend what he builds. But then as he lifts his gaze from the pedestal he sees above and beyond it the triangle which symbolizes the eternal God Who presides over all.

He is in fact looking at a picture which summarizes the teaching of the Royal Arch that we must worship our Creator in such manner as our religion may instruct us and do His work in this world with a perception and perspective set always in the context of eternity. And here we find again that continued contrast which exists between Craft and Chapter. When the candidate in the Craft is restored to light he sees the Great Lights which will guide his terrestrial progress; in the Royal Arch his attention is at once focused on the eternal. In the three Craft degrees he has been led through 'the intricate windings of this mortal life' to 'the closing hour of existence'; now, his first vision as a Companion is directed to penetrating the mysterious veil and to realizing that the Order is, as he will later be reminded, 'intimately blended with all that is nearest and dearest to us in a future state of existence'. The Craft requires him to follow the teaching of his religion here on earth; the Chapter reminds him that he lives and practises that teaching in the context of eternity.

That however is not all. The path he travels will have its perils and disappointments; but on his way he will be guided by those who now line his road. He is not alone but has Companions for his journey; he has become their Companion as they have become his.

All too quickly the moment passes. He reads the scroll, is reminded that light is the creation of the Grand Architect, and retires.

You will have noticed that phrase 'the Grand Architect'; those were the words originally used in the Royal Arch and that is what the initials on your Grand Chapter certificate stand for. It is a form of address which by a slight difference in wording stresses that while the Royal Arch is the completion of the Master Mason's degree it is also a separate and distinct Order, looking beyond our earthly existence to the eternity in which it is set and to the Creator Who gives it form and substance.

I have tried to describe what one moment in our ceremonies means to me and why I feel that it is so important. It arises from the ritual and the rubric but they alone cannot communicate the message it should convey. This one moment which can mean so much and provide so much on which to meditate and indeed on which to rely for support, achieves its greatest meaning only then those involved in it realize that they are each one a part of the whole and are depicting a mystery. Be mindful of this when you welcome a new candidate to the light of our Order and do your best to make the experience something for him to remember, something which can become increasingly meaningful to him as he progresses in the Royal Arch and as he journeys through life. Never allow the magic of the moment to be lost because you have not played your part in it to the best of your ability.

7
'THE ANTIENT TOAST' (1982)

*An after-dinner catechism (sometimes known as 'the antient toast')
provided some thoughts for the centenary meeting. The words quoted
from the Apocrypha (Ecclesiasticus, chapter 44), were later set to
music for an anthem as part of the celebrations of the centenary of a
Lodge in Kettering. This was done by a non-mason, Christopher
Gower, Master of the Music at Peterborough Cathedral, another
instance of our indebtedness to the ecclesiastical establishment of the
Diocese.*

AS YOU WILL have read in the histories, this Royal Arch Province
was constituted on 10 June 1880, with the Provincial Grand Master,
his Grace the Duke of Manchester, as the first Grand Superintendent.
But since it was not until 1882 that he held his first Provincial Convocation we are keeping the anniversary in 1982.

At this centenary meeting we honour particularly the memory of
those who established Royal Arch Masonry in the Province; but we
think too of those who followed them and continued to build on the
foundation that had been so carefully laid. It is because of the efforts
of all these Companions that this Supreme Order has become what it
is today in our Province, happy, lively, flourishing; proud of its past
and confident for its future. And we are determined that it shall so
remain and be handed on to our successors in good heart, that they too
may know the companionship we know, and share in their turn the
aims of Royal Arch Masonry.

At the start of the ceremony of Exaltation we pray that the candidate may ever remember that the object of our Institution is the welfare of our fellow creatures, but above all the honour and glory of
God. It was with these aims in view that our predecessors worked to
build up this Province. Our duty to them and to our successors is to
continue the work of building, laying a course that will support what
is to follow; generations past, present and future working together as
Companions in that peace, love and unity which we shall recall as we
sing 'Peace, Love and Harmony' together before we part.

So while we celebrate the past we think too of our own role in the work and of the role that those who will follow us will play. This, for me, is the real meaning of a part of our ceremonial which takes place after the Chapter has been closed and in the convivial atmosphere of the refectory, when we praise the famous men of our own tradition, honouring them in the Antient Toast: Moses, Aholiab and Bezeleel; Solomon king of Israel, Hiram king of Tyre and Hiram Abif; Zerubbabel prince of the people, Haggai the prophet and Joshua or Jeshua the son of Josadek, the High Priest.

And here once again we find that great difference between the Craft and Royal Arch of which I have pointed to examples before in these addresses, the difference between the temporal and the eternal. In the Craft the legend tells of the building of king Solomon's Temple, a structure magnificent in its time and the first permanent resting place for the Ark of the Covenant; but this covers only one brief moment in history. In the Royal Arch, in the Antient Toast, we recognize that moment as but one part of a greater story, that of man's quest for a knowledge of God and of his everlasting purposes. So here again we see how the Royal Arch penetrates further and deeper than the Craft, setting a frame for Freemasonry within the context of eternity and the teachings of religion.

The author of the book of Ecclesiasticus in the Aprocrypha recognized how past, present and future are linked together and dependent on each other when he wrote:

'Let us now praise famous men, and our fathers that begat us . . . Such as did bear rule in their kingdoms, men renowned for their power, giving counsel by their understanding and declaring prophecies; leaders of the people by their counsels, and by their knowledge of learning meet for the people, wise and eloquent in their instructions . . . All these were honoured in their generations, and were the glory of their times.

There be of them that have left a name behind them, that their praises might be reported. And some there be, which have no memorial; and are become as though they had never been born, and their children after them. But these were merciful men, whose righteousness hath not been forgotten.

With their seed shall continually remain a good inheritance, and their children are within the covenant. Their seed shall remain for ever and their glory shall not be blotted out. Their bodies are buried in peace, but their name liveth for evermore[1]'.

Now look for a moment at those whom we commemorate by name in the Antient Toast and see how truly the author of that passage wrote.

Moses was 'the man of God', the leader who brought the Children of Israel out of captivity; Bezeleel was 'filled with the spirit of God, in wisdom and in understanding, and in knowledge, and in all manner of workmanship'; Aholiab was of the tribe of Dan and a skilled worker who was set apart to be a teacher: one 'leader of the people by his counsels'; two who 'have no memorial'.

Solomon was of course a great king; Hiram was king of a rich and powerful city known probably over a wider area than was Jerusalem at the time since it was a strong sea-power in the Mediterranean; and Hiram Abif, the widow's son, was 'the son of a woman of the daughters of Dan, and his father was a man of Tyre; skilful in gold, and in silver, in brass, in iron, in stone, and in timber, in purple, in blue and in fine linen and in crimson': two great kings 'such as did bear rule in their kingdoms, men renowned for their power' of whom only one truly 'left a name behind him' and a widow's son 'with knowledge of learning meet for the people' wise in instruction, to whom the work was to bring honour and death in an alien land.

Lastly, Zerubbabel, Haggai and Joshua; a prince of the house of David who had served in the bodyguard of Darius, king of Persia; Haggai the prophet who had brought to his prince the Lord's command to rebuild the Temple; and Joshua, the High Priest, successor to Aaron the brother of Moses, charged with the oversight of the sacred mysteries of the Jewish religion. A prince, a mystic and a priest, 'giving counsel by their understanding and declaring prophesies; leaders of the people by their counsels'.

Not all of these were great or famous by the standards of history; yet all were 'honoured in their generation and were the glory of their times'; each played his part as a leader in carrying forward the grand design begun under Moses, doing the work of his generation that future generations might honour, approach and worship their Creator.

But remember too that each trio was aided by a multitude of others without whose skill and industry the work would not have been completed, men of whom we know nothing, the kind of men who worked together as companions at the rebuilding of Jerusalem after the captivity 'with the trowel in their hand and the sword by their side' and who now are 'become as though they had never been born' — the kind of men of whom the late Bro Rudyard Kipling wrote in these lines:

'Let us now praise famous men,
Men of little showing;
For their work continueth,
And their work continueth,
Broad and deep continueth,
Greater than their knowing'[2]

When you honour the Antient Toast think of such men too and remember with gratitude and great humility the many who have worked in this Province and in your own Chapter to build soundly and well that you may enjoy Royal Arch Masonry and may have a secure foundation on which to build for the next century; and resolve to build soundly in your turn that your successors too may have a goodly inheritance.

[1] From *Ecclesiasticus*, 44: 1-14 (Authorised Version).
[2] *Stalky & Co*: A School Song.

8
'COMPANIONS' (1983)

The Holy Royal Arch is said to be the completion of the Third Degree; yet its members are not 'Brethren' but 'Companions'. There must be a reason; and what does the name imply? This had been touched on in 1981 (Chapter 6) but needed further thought.

GRAND LODGE and Grand Chapter rule separate and distinct Orders. Yet in spite of this the Craft and the Royal Arch are linked virtually inextricably, for as we are reminded by the Preamble to the Craft Constitutions, the Act of Union sealed in December 1813 between the two Grand Lodges which formed the United Grand Lodge, the Premier Grand Lodge and the Grand Lodge of the 'Antients', 'declared and pronounced that pure Ancient Masonry consists of three degrees, and no more; *viz* those of the Entered Apprentice, the Fellow Craft, and the Master Mason, including the Supreme Order of the Holy Royal Arch . . .'

Yet the candidate who has just been conducted through the ceremony of Exaltation and now stands[1] in the West of the Chapter wearing his new regalia for the first time, clothed in the robe of innocence and looking at a scene more splendid in colour and contrast than any he has met in the Craft, may well feel that he has encountered something quite different and distinct from Freemasonry as he has hitherto known it. Even the time-scale of the narrative has advanced some 500 years from the death of Hiram and King Solomon's dedication of the first Temple. He may indeed be imagining that he has taken a fourth degree in Freemasonry and it is right that this impression should be firmly corrected. 'Such' he is told 'is not the case. It is the Master Mason's completed'.

But it is difficult for us to remember always how important this link is and that the Royal Arch does not stand on its own. Laurence Dermott, the second and most famous of the Grand Secretaries of the 'Antients', called it 'the root, heart and marrow of Masonry'; but the root cannot prosper unless it is nourished, nor can the heart or marrow exist without the body. The Craft is as necessary to the Royal Arch as the Royal Arch is to the Craft.

In our love for the beautiful ceremony of Exaltation, in our realization of the deeper and richer philosophy of the Chapter ritual, and in our appreciation of the companionship which is so vital a part of Royal Arch Masonry we may sometimes forget that the basis of Craft Freemasonry is also the basis for our own Order.

You all know the principles on which we are taught that Freemasonry rests, 'brotherly love, relief and truth'. The Most Worshipful the Grand Master spoke simply but profoundly about them at the Annual Investiture in 1982 and reminded us once again of their meaning for the 'speculative' Freemason of today[2]; and we as Royal Arch Masons must practise them, the more so since we call ourselves 'Companions'.

That word 'Companion' referred originally to soldiers who shared their bread together, messmates. Your Companion was therefore the man with whom you fed in the barracks and beside whom you fought in the field; the man who defended you in battle as you would defend him; the man on whom your very life might depend, as might his on you. To be a Companion was and is much more than to be a Brother. Perhaps that is why our Chapters have no officer equivalent to the Almoner of the Craft, because it is the task of each of us to look after his Companion. But this does make demands on our time and our talents which we are not always ready to meet. I sometimes think that if there is a masonic vice it is a tendency to see such things too much in terms of cash (cheque-book charity) and too little in terms of service, something which hardly accords with the bond and boast of Companionship.

This common responsibility is all of a piece with the exhortation we hear at every Craft Installation, that we should so conduct ourselves that the world (and that means the whole world, not just our brethren) will regard a Freemason as 'one to whom the burdened heart may pour forth its sorrow' and 'whose heart is expanded by benevolence' for as the Address to the Principals[3] reminds us in our own Order 'the public reputation of the Institution will generally be found to reflect the character and conduct of its principal officers' and I may add that the character and companionship of the Chapter will also reflect their attitude and effort.

In the Chapter, as in the Lodge, it is for the rulers to set the example and provide the impetus. Specifically, in the Chapter this is the duty of the Principals who 'when in Chapter assembled are to be considered conjointly as the Master, and each severally as a Master'[4]; but above all it is the duty of the First Principal as the leader of the team, the driving force, and he it is who must see that the companionship of the Chapter is a reality for all its members. So if a Companion is absent from Chapter he should make sure that a message reaches the absentee to tell him he was missed, to hope that he will be present at the next meeting, and of course to offer help and comfort when help or comfort is needed. We can hardly call ourselves Companions if we do not look after our members in this way.

And here let me remind you that masonic rank has nothing to do with this. The duty arises and exists because we are Companions. In common with every other Grand Superintendent I have to confer ranks, with differing degrees of precedence and it is one of the most difficult duties that we have. It is not those ranks that make us Companions; and where I am able to honour any one of you I am placing on him the burden and the privilege of service, of expressing the Companionship of the Order in yet greater degree. But in the fundamental analysis we are all Companions, each concerned for each; and in that lies our strength for this is as true for the newly exalted Companion as for the most senior member of your Chapter.

So when you hear your new Companion told that the ceremony through which he has just passed has completed his Third Degree let it remind you that though we have a deeper philosophy than our brethren in the Craft who have not yet been exalted into the Royal Arch, we too rest on the basis of brotherly love, relief and truth; but that we, as the proud inheritors of the ancient title of Companion, with all its implications of mutual help and support, owe an even greater duty to each other; and that each one of us is in a very real sense the Almoner of the Chapter under the leadership and direction of its First Principal.

But taking the Royal Arch seriously, as we must do, will not prevent our meetings from being happy, cheerful and relaxed; rather it should enhance our pleasure in them. So do enjoy your Royal Arch meetings, and see that your Companions enjoy them too, both in Chapter and afterwards in the refectory.

---

[1] In some workings this Address is given at a different point in the ceremony; but the principle is the same.
[2] Minutes of United Grand Lodge of England, Quarterly Communication, 30 April 1980, pp 34-5.
[3] As given in the *Perfect Ceremonies* working.
[4] Supreme Grand Chapter Regulations, No 48.

9
'VEILED IN ALLEGORY' (1984)

It was time to take stock, providentially as matters turned out; over the next four years it became necessary to consider the attitude taken by certain Christian churches towards Freemasonry and to concentrate on their criticisms, which many Freemasons felt were misconceived. Certainly many brethren who were actively supporting their churches were deeply hurt by the lack of understanding and sympathy which they felt was apparent. The problem was not so much to deal with the criticisms — that could be left to others; it was rather to help our own people to understand, and to prevent them from withdrawing the help they were giving their churches unless of course they were asked to do so, as happened in a very few cases. But at the time when this address was delivered all that was in the future.

THERE ARE MANY definitions of Freemasonry but the one which appears in the ritual and is known at least to every Fellow Craft is 'a peculiar system of morality, veiled in allegory and illustrated by symbols'. In the old eighteenth century workings the morality was inculcated by the ritual while the allegories and symbols were explained in the lectures. Unhappily, the lectures, not having been revised for a century and a half, have fallen into disuse except as exhibition pieces. This is a great pity because today, when man has the power to make a paradise or a desert of the earth, we have more need than ever before in that earth's history to discover and clarify the truths for which we stand and which are the basis of our moral code. That is why in these addresses I try to direct your attention to some of the symbols and allegories with which Freemasonry in general and the Royal Arch in particular abound. I would emphatically urge each of you to study our Order and note for yourself those symbols and allegories which you find instructive; and do not be afraid to share them with your Companions. None of us can afford to ignore another's help in dealing with the moral puzzles with which life abounds today. Outward appearance is a veneer, and the man does not exist who at heart does not at times feel inadequate and lost however little he may show it. True symbols and allegories help because they explain the perspective of an undiscoverable eternity in terms of the three-dimensioned world in which we live. It is to this relationship with eternity that the Royal Arch directs your attention though it goes no further; you must look to your religion to learn more.

Now a strange thing about that definition of Freemasonry is that almost everyone places the emphasis on the signs and symbols; yet they are not actually part of the definition but only an explanation of the method of teaching. The actual definition is 'a system of morality' and that as we know is based on brotherly love, relief and truth and not, as so often in the outside world, on the uncharitable conviction of one's own superior worth or judgment. The allegory and symbol are the ways in which that basis is taught; it is illustrated, or made clear, by symbols; it is hidden, or veiled, in allegory. It is that veil to which I particularly wish to draw your attention today.

Think for a moment about the discovery made by the Sojourners. They stood together on the brink of cavity, staring down into darkness, knowing it must be explored but ignorant of what danger might be there. For all three to descend would be folly; prudence and practicality alike dictated that two should remain above ground; one must be lowered alone, trusting his life to his companions. None was willing to hold back, 'being aware that the architect of the former building had designed no part of it in vain'; all wished to go on. So they drew lots. With due precaution one then descended. He returned with a scroll; they examined it together in the light and found it contained the record of God's commands and promises to man. With his imagination fired by this discovery the Sojourner descended again as the sun rose to its zenith; this time he could see that he stood in a vault in the middle of which was a veiled altar with peculiar symbols on its side. He knew he was in the presence of something mysterious and holy. Superstition and dread would make him doubt whether he was worthy to lift that veil and we do not know how long he stood there before he dared to approach and raise it, to find that he was gazing at something so holy that he dared not reveal it even at the command of his prince and the High Priest.

This story is of course high drama, and none the worse for that. But it so catches the imagination that we can lose ourselves in the narrative without seeking to discover what lesson it holds. The altar was only found after a lonely venture into the unknown; when found its secret was veiled and the Sojourner had to dare to raise that veil of his own volition before he could comprehend the treasure it concealed.

It is such allegories as this that are the real jewels of Freemasonry. If it were merely a system of words to be spoken and actions to be performed before a critical audience anxious only to assess the perfection of word and gesture, it would long ago have foundered under 'the destroying hand of time'. This is one reason why I try to emphasize that ritual is a method of orderly teaching, a civil politeness to candidates so that they may receive instruction, and of keeping order and dignity in our proceedings; it is not an end in itself but only a means to an end. What matters is the message; the words convey the message and must be learnt for that reason. But if Freemasonry had been only an affair of ritual word and gesture without hidden meaning, few men of intelligence would have been prepared to sit by night after night and listen to the repetition, over and over again, of the same set of sounds.

I must make it clear that I am neither criticizing nor decrying ritual. A message has to be communicated to the candidate, fully, in due order, with propriety and dignity. The ritual shows us how to effect this. Variations rarely improve it or (and this is the important thing) clarify it for the candidate. Mumbled or badly learned ritual, or poor presentation may well mean that the message is not even understood on that first and most important occasion when the candidate is at his most receptive; unless the meaning and the words have been mastered or at least carefully considered by the speaker the candidate is unlikely even to perceive the veil of allegory, much less be encouraged to lift that veil for himself. Good ritual, even though not word-perfect, is a delight to us all and can be a real source of inspiration to candidates; word-perfect ritual delivered without meaning or understanding is boring to the observer and carries neither challenge nor encouragement for him to whom it should be addressed. It is not the plaudits or criticisms of the Past Principals which spell success or failure but the clarity with which the message has been conveyed. Part of that success will depend on the candidate realizing that he is indeed being instructed in a 'system of morality' but much more will depend on this being done in a way that he becomes eager to learn more, to lift the veil, to explore the symbolism and allegory for himself; that is in fact what we mean by 'a daily advancement in masonic knowledge', a phrase too often used to imply a daily or even weekly glance at a book of ritual. Some never do try to lift the veil; but there are many who do realize that there is more to Freemasonry than the idle repetition of a patter of words and would welcome the help of their Companions in discovering these hidden meanings. The Explanation of the First Tracing Board is a good starting point and I commend it to you; and the lectures of the Royal Arch, as ever, carry the Craft teaching forward to penetrate the veil of eternity.

Companions, I do urge you never to underestimate the thirst for masonic knowledge which so many of those who come into our Order feel. Only by thinking about the message and meaning that lie behind the ritual and by discovering the symbols and unveiling the allegories for yourself after the manner of that first Sojourner can you become able to satisfy that thirst. But when you have searched them out you will not only be able to help your Brother and Companion, you will also have learnt lessons for yourself; and by expounding the true ideals of Freemasonry you will be ensuring that it survives for the benefit of generations yet unborn.

10
'IF FREEMASONRY IS NOT A RELIGION ... (1985)

From 1985 to 1988 the dominant theme in masonic thought in Eng-land was the relationship between Freemasonry and religion, particu-larly Christianity. In such matters emotion can obscure issues; many, probably most, Freemasons feel deeply about what one might term the ethos of the Order and most active Christians, clerical and lay, are deeply committed to their Faith. Christian Freemasons were greatly distressed by what they saw as misapprehensions and even in some cases active misrepresentations about the Craft. It was important not only to acknowledge this distress but also that Freemasons at least should understand both points of view and should not feel compelled to withdraw from their churches unless the minister wished them to do so; it was on the whole unlikely that they would wish to withdraw from the Craft.

In the event it was found that many ministers recognized the work done in their churches by masonic members and few Freemasons either felt it necessary or were asked to resign from church duties, nor did the Lodges in the Provinces lose many members over this. Our losses in my Province could be counted on the fingers of one hand.

Another problem was of course to explain the situation to widows and others who were distressed by what appeared to be attacks on the memory of those near and dear to them, as well as to any wives who might be induced by these thunderings and misrepresentations to feel that their husbands were engaged in a discreditable or dangerous pursuit. The only possible course was to try to restore understanding and perspective while seeking to explain the views of our critics. We could never hope to convince the bigots, but patient explanation could be helpful to both sides. It was to these purposes that this address was directed.

FROM TIME TO time any great movement will find itself under attack. The motives of the attackers will vary, but bigotry (by which I mean a conviction not just that one narrow view is good but that all others are actively wrong), suspicion and fear are generally high on the list and in such cases, however unfounded the basis of the attack may seem to be, the onslaught must be treated with respect because it arises on the whole from honestly held views. But when an attack starts in such a way there have always been those who will join in from more sinister motives such as envy, greed or political gain; and when this happens it is only too easy for the victim to be diverted from dealing with the main dispute to tackle this more malicious and wounding witch-hunt (for that is what it becomes) and so perhaps win a battle but lose the war.

Freemasonry has no immunity from such attacks, as we all know; and because we are happy in our fraternity we consider them unjustifiable. But we do have to make that distinction between attacks honestly motivated and others, and we do have to be clear what it is that we are fighting. In this connection I want to consider particularly recent pronouncements which seek to imply that there is an inconsistency between religion and Freemasonry, or that Freemasonry itself is a religion, which it is not.

In such cases we are confronted initially by those who, quite sincerely, hold that there is something in Freemasonry that is inconsistent with the theology of their particular religious belief, and it would be wrong to dismiss their concern as arising otherwise than from honestly held conviction. We must try to understand what they are saying; only then can we consider their arguments and decide whether we think they are right or wrong, and if wrong why we believe those arguments to be unsound. Basically, as I understand it, these critics are saying that Freemasonry is so akin to a religion that it requires a belief in a Supreme Being Who is not the God in Whom they believe. This seems to be claiming that we as Freemasons worship some particular god of our own, which would indeed be heresy to a Christian, but which we know is not true; in fact it confuses morality with religion, a subject to which I will return.

So you see how important it is that each of us should be quite sure that he knows what Freemasonry is. We maintain and have consistently proclaimed that it is not a religion. It does require that a man shall have some form of religious belief in that every candidate must confirm that he believes in a Supreme Being but it does not presume to do more, except to require that every Freemason must practise the religion he professes. That religion may be Christianity, Judaism or any other. But without such a belief a man cannot become a Freemason. So that in fact you must profess a religion before you enter the Craft and continue to practise your religion after being initiated, which for me makes it difficult to understand how it can be claimed that you acquire a religion by becoming a Freemason.

So, if Freemasonry is not a religion, what is it? Each of us knows the answer and it should be well understood by anyone who has taken the trouble to look dispassionately at the facts. It is a system of morality and, as Dr Oliver said, 'morality is not the groundwork, but the result and fruit of religion'. Yet so determined are some of those who are attacking us that they accuse us of being a quasi-religion, something which to me is a contradiction in terms. It is a sad thing when followers of Christ can accuse fellow-Christians of behaviour incompatible with their religion because they belong to a fraternity which inculcates a morality founded on brotherly love, relief and truth, and teaches that a man must do his duty to his God, to his neighbour and himself. Unfortunately history shows such accusations can easily be made in the name of religion, even in that of a religion whose Founder consorted with the outcasts and told the parable of the Good Samaritan. But sad though it is, history also shows us how important dogmatic opinions are both to those who profess them and to those who oppose them. We as Freemasons must not be caught in the trap of trying to reconcile or support differing dogmas in this way, a trap the destructive power of which was one of the reasons for the prohibition against discussion of religious differences in Lodge as being inimical to harmony and brotherly love.

Freemasons then may profess differing religions but nevertheless do accept one code of morality. There is no inconsistency in this, for the morality which we teach is based on our duty in love and charity to our fellows, something which is common to all the great religions; beyond that we do not go. Our teachings are indeed based on allegories which are founded on the Old Testament, itself included in the Christian Bible; and we all know that in other masonic Orders that teaching in fact becomes Christian though, while many of us are members of them, they are not accepted as part of pure ancient Freemasonry.

There is an allegory in our Royal Arch ceremonies which forcibly brings home to me the relationship between religion and morality. It occurs both during the Exaltation ceremony at its most impressive part and during the Closing, when the Principals hold up their sceptres in the form of a triangle. From the apex, the part which is symbolically nearest Heaven, the emblems of prophecy and priesthood are extended, signifying God's relationship to man, expressed through the revelations of prophetic teaching on the one hand and on the other through the ordered worship by which each of us approaches his Creator in accordance with the practices of his religion. At the foot of the space thus defined lies the sceptre of the First Principal, the symbol of our earthly existence, showing how for every Royal Arch Companion the bounds of his behaviour are limited and defined by the revelation and practice of his religion. Together these three form a triangle capable of withstanding attack from any direction because each part of it supports and gives strength to the rest.

That is how I see the relationship in allegory; and as a practising Christian, just as I can find no incompatibility between our morality and my religion, so I see nothing incompatible between my religion and my Freemasonry; nor, in the light of the teachings of Christ, can I see that being prepared to pray in the company of those who worship in some other way is a form of heresy. Some words which Dr Oliver, himself both priest and mason, once wrote are in point here, 'No matter what may be the birth, language or colour of the skin, every man is a brother if he faithfully performs his duty to God, his neighbour and himself'[1]; and again, 'I will admit my Hebrew brother into a mason's lodge . . . but as he will not abandon his faith at my command, neither will I[2]'. The parallel will be obvious to you.

Be of good cheer, Companions. Remember that Horace Walpole, said to be a Freemason, wrote at a time when Freemasonry was in the doldrums, 'I believe that nothing but a persecution could bring [it] into vogue again'. This fracas will have made us think about Freemasonry and about religion and we shall be the better for it. Meanwhile, let us continue to conduct ourselves in accordance with the principles of our Order so well summarized in the Charge after Initiation and the Addresses to the Master and the Brethren at Installations, always remembering to think of these principles, since we are not merely Brothers but Companions of the Royal Arch, in the context of eternity and in the light of that Companionship of which we are so proud. I commend to you also the pronouncement on Freemasonry and religion accepted in Grand Lodge[3], and I ask you to study it carefully[4]. But it is by precept and example in our daily lives, at home and at work, in hours of relaxation and of toil, as well as at church, chapel, synagogue or temple, that we shall convince the doubters and prove to the world that there is no incompatibility between religion and Freemasonry, that our morality exists in the context of religion and that indeed a man is a better follower of his religion because he is a Freemason.

[1] *The Symbol of Glory*, Valedictory Address (1850).
[2] *ibid*.
[3] The resolution is reproduced at Appendix C.
[4] The relationship between Freemasonry and religion is summarized in a Grand Lodge pamphlet *Freemasonry and Religion*, reproduced at Appendix D.

11
BUILDING FOR THE FUTURE (1986)

Criticism is always wounding to some degree, even when well meant, and by no means all that which was being directed at the Craft was well-intentioned though some of it was sincere. The natural reaction to hurt pride is one of anger but it is more sensible to try to think whether and to what extent the critics may have reason on their side. This involves questioning the fundamentals on which our own conduct is based. There were therefore two things to be done in the situation which faced us in the mid-eighties; first, we had to determine what were the fundamentals for which we stood and second, we had to distinguish genuine criticism from that put forward from more questionable motives. This address sought to suggest points from which the first of these could be established.

I WOULD HOPE that by now you have all had time to recover from the surprise and sense of shock which recent attacks on Freemasonry may have induced, particularly those from sources we have every right to feel should at least be sympathetic to our ideals. Many of those who have joined in them may have been well meaning according to their lights; more have been misinformed and some I fear, have been deliberately misleading, not always without ulterior motive. There has even been at times an air of gloating in some quarters where one might have expected understanding or at least compassion. For our part, we have tried to meet our detractors with reason and explanation and, may I say, with a charity they have not always extended to us; we can reasonably feel that we have answered their questions even if they have elected not to hear. Now it is time to take stock and look ahead.

I think that we at least have learnt something from all this. We have been forced took dispassionately at a part of our lives which has meant and does mean much to each of us. I believe we will each have come to the conclusion that we have nothing of importance for which

47

to reproach ourselves other than perhaps too great a tendency to be reticent about our membership of the Craft and about its aims and principles — something which arises from our wish to enjoy the privacy normally accorded to private clubs and gatherings. Perhaps our own reticence has indeed been one reason why some of our critics may have felt that we had indeed something discreditable to hide.

In some matters such as the penalties attached to the Obligations and that of the second word in our own Order it may be expedient to take some action. But I believe that apart from such action it is now time for us to put these things behind us in order to think and plan constructively for the future, though remembering with gratitude the work done by those who have toiled so hard on our behalf and encouraging them to continue in their efforts. We can safely leave to them matters of high policy such as public relations, and do our part by acting according to the tenets of our Craft. Nevertheless, while taking stock it will be as well to think of basic principles and each of us should make certain that he is quite clear in his own mind about what those principles are, with particular reference in our own case to this Order.

On what basis then are we to build our future as a fraternity? Surely on that which over so many years has brought the message of brotherly love, relief and truth to us all. In that respect nothing has altered except perhaps that we have rightly checked any tendency there may have been to blur the line between Freemasonry and religion. We stand firm on our basic principles, never interfering in any masonic capacity with a brother's religious beliefs but refusing to admit anyone who does not confess a belief in a Supreme Being, requiring a high standard of morality from every brother, inculcating the virtues of compassion, benevolence and charity not only towards our own members but to all mankind, dropping the tear of sympathy over the failings of a brother and 'pouring the healing balm of consolation into the bosom of the afflicted'.

But for Companions of the Royal Arch there is more. We are reminded every time we enter a Royal Arch Chapter of the framework in which the teaching of the Order is set because there in the centre of the room stands the pedestal on which is set the Ineffable Name of God as it was revealed to Moses, placed on the emblem of eternity. Our detractors have pointed to the fact that in some rituals this pedestal has been called an altar as evidence that we are practising a religion, once again misunderstanding us either wilfully or through ignorance. It is of course no such thing; it is a reminder to us that the Sojourners found an altar of which this is a representation, and of the fact that a Royal Arch Companion views the lessons of the Craft in the light of the eternal rather than of this worldly existence, that, as in the Craft, he is expected to reverence his God and practise his religion. On it, as on that altar, the Ineffable Name is placed, a Name which as our critics well know is derived from the Holy Bible, the Name our reverence of which justifies the use of the word 'Holy' in the title of our Order.

The very shape of that pedestal has a message for us. It represents a double cube of wrought stone, a perfect ashlar, for the term applies to any stone which has been worked and smoothed ready to take its place in the building even though it is not a perfect cube with all sides equal. We are all familiar with the words used in the Lectures and in the Explanation of the First Degree Tracing Board to describe such a stone — 'a stone of a true die or square, fit only to be tried by the square and compasses'. So to the speculative Freemason the perfect ashlar represents, in the words of the ritual, 'a regular well-spent life in acts of piety and virtue' since the square represents morality while the compasses remind us of the justice of God.

Only on such a stone and on the emblem of eternity can we presume to place the Ineffable Name; and we show our respect for it by gestures which seal our fidelity to the teachings of our Creator in whatever form we worship Him, while humbly acknowledging that we are not worthy to look upon Him.

This pedestal then epitomises the difference between the Craft and the Royal Arch, at once united in the Master Mason's Degree yet separated by that which marks the difference between Brother and Companion and by our insistence that every part of our earthly pilgrimage is conditioned and governed by the eternity in which it is framed. And so it is that as in life you do not choose your brother but do select your friend, so in 'pure ancient Masonry', though you come into a fraternity where you may not know all the brethren of the Lodge you enter and will certainly have little knowledge of what to expect, you are admitted into a Chapter among Companions many of whom you will already know, and with a basic knowledge of Freemasonry.

We as Companions of this Order are of course anxious to bring brethren into its companionship. We must however be sure that those whom we would seek to introduce will in due time appreciate the serious side of its teaching. Many a brother will come forward for exaltation because the sense of loss and failure which are endemic in the Third Degree leave him with a feeling of dissatisfaction, and because he is told that the genuine secrets of a Master Mason are only to be learnt in the Chapter. He will only remain to learn the deeper meaning of our teaching if he finds himself truly accepted as a Companion and in a happy gathering. We do have a serious message in the Royal

Arch; but we can still learn from the Craft and strive to unite in the grand design of 'being happy and communicating happiness'; and remember that you cannot achieve the one without practising the other. As I have often said before, 'enjoy your Masonry'; by doing so you will be helping others not only to enjoy but to understand it, both in Craft and Royal Arch.

Plate 1

*Cadwallader, 9th Lord Blaney (1720-1765) the First Grand Principal or 'Grand Master Z' of the
Royal Arch of Jerusalem. He was Grand Master of the premier Grand Lodge (the Moderns) when
the Royal Grand Chapter was formed by the Charter of Compact in 1766.*

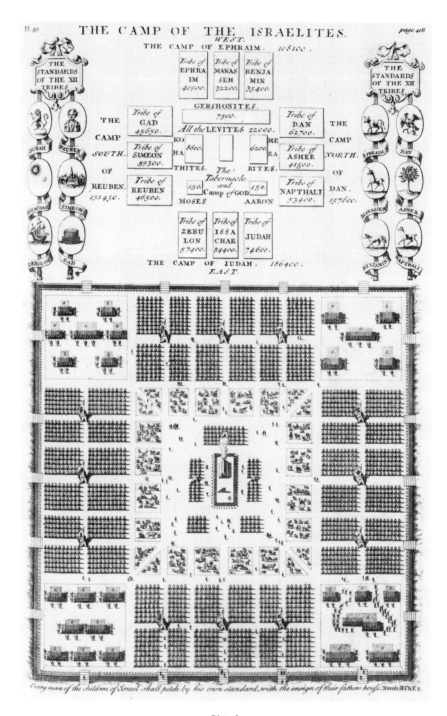

Plate 2
The Camp of the Israelites under the banners of Reuben (man), Judah (lion), Ephraim (ox) and Dan (eagle) with the ensigns of the Twelve tribes.

Plate 3
Above: The Arms of the Antients Grand Lodge and right, the United Grand Lodge of England which include the Man, Lion, Ox and Eagle.

Plate 4
The four principal banners of the Royal Arch depict the Man (Reuben), the Lion (Judah), the Ox (Ephraim), the Eagle (Dan) and the four camps of the Israelites (opposite).

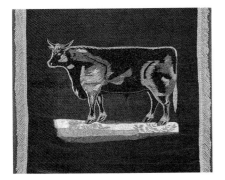

Plate 5
The ensigns of the twelve tribes of the Israelites to be seen on the staves in a Royal Arch Chapter arrangement (see Plate 8).

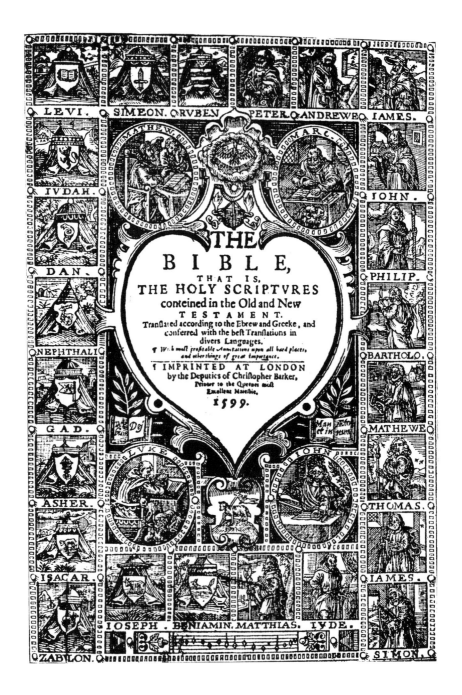

Plate 6
The title page from the 1599 'Barker Bible'.

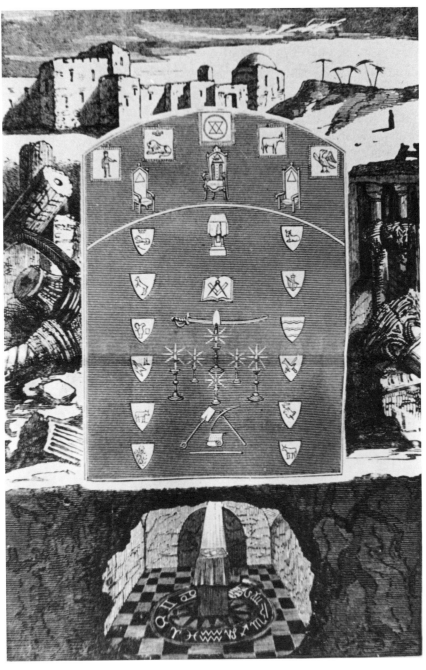

Plate 7
A Royal Arch tracing board from the 1884 edition of the Oxford Royal Arch Ritual.

Plate 8
The arrangement of a Royal Arch Chapter with the four principal banners, twelve ensigns on staves, the implements and the Pedestal.

Plate 9
A present day Companions' apron with the triple tau emblem inside the triangle.

Plate 10
*An old apron with T over H (*Templum Heirosolyma*) which later became the triple tau.*

Plate 11
A Royal Arch model still used by the 1808 Albany Chapter No 151 in Newport, Isle of Wight.

Plate 12
A present day pedestal.

Plate 13
The earliest 'Grand Lodge Royal Arch Certificate' of 1792 which was used until the latest one dated 1816. It is thought to have been designed by John Perkins, a member of the Antients' Domatic Lodge No 234.

Plate 14
An old model of a dome with removable stones for use during Royal Arch ceremonies at the Masonic Hall, Abergavenny in Wales.

Plate 15
Present day implements of the crow, pick and shovel, the platonic bodies and Principals' sceptres.

Plate 16
*The Revd. George Oliver, D.D. (1782-1867), as Deputy Provincial Grand Master of Lincolnshire.
Initiated c.1802 in Peterborough while still a minor, his father kneeling beside him as guarantor, he
became a prolific masonic author greatly respected in the 19th century. His story is told in* Priest
and Freemason *by the present author.*

Plate 17
The Great Banners of the Supreme Grand Chapter of Royal Arch Masons of Scotland. Above: The Crimson Banner with the ensigns of the twelve tribes, and the four headed animals. Below: The Scottish Green Banner with the signs of the Zodiac.

Plate 18
A rare and decorated 18th century Antients apron showing several Royal Arch emblems as well as those of other degrees worked in lodges before the Union.
An old painted satin Royal Arch apron. The three Principals are accompanied by three officers wearing college caps.

Plate 19
A rare 18th century Royal Arch Principal's jewel.

Plate 20
A Royal Arch Scottish jewel of 1868.

A companion's jewel.

A Past First Principal's jewel.

An Irish Past King's jewel.

Plate 21

A Scottish Companion's jewel.

A Scottish First Grand Principal's jewel.

A Scottish jewel of the Third Grand Principal.

Plate 22
The Chapter Room at the Masonic Hall in Bristol. Above: Facing east showing the twelve ensigns and the pedestal. Below: Facing west towards the organ pipes.

12
COMPATIBILITY (1987)

In 1987 Provincial Grand Chapter was held on 2 June. Earlier in the month a working party of the General Synod of the Church of England had produced a report on Freemasonry and this was to be discussed at the Synod in July[1]. The Report queried the compatibility of Freemasonry and Christianity and was of course seized on by the Press as condemnatory of the Craft though the members of the Working Party denied that it went so far. Reading it as a layman I felt little sympathy with what seemed to be a very narrow and exclusive theological argument, very different for instance from that shown in such documents as 'Towards a Theology for Inter-Faith Dialogue', a discussion paper for the impending Lambeth Conference[2]; nor I fear did the Report itself impress; its journalistic style and use of exclamation marks, its unnecessary and inappropriate descents into ridicule and more seriously its apparently ambivalent approach to the important and serious question of inter-faith prayer and theology, seemed out of place in a serious public document. While some Freemasons would doubtless read it, the majority would only see Press reports which in general suggested and indeed in some cases stated outright that it condemned Freemasonry in general and the Royal Arch in particular as blasphemous. The conduct of the Craft's case was of course in the hands of those appointed by the Grand Master and Grand Lodge for the purpose but my responsibility to the brethren of my Province was surely to give what guidance I could in what must be a disturbing time; so the address already prepared for the 1987 meeting was scrapped in favour of that which follows.

This address had to be delivered before the Synod debate took place but there seems no reason now to revise it though on reflection it was perhaps too kind to the working party's document. As to the outcome it seems to be generally agreed that Freemasonry won the debate in the General Synod but lost the vote because the political groupings in the Synod made it certain that the Report would be accepted; and though it was rather half-heartedly asserted to be a basis for on-going dialogue, its final paragraph alleged that in the opinion of the majority of the working party there were 'a number of very fundamental reasons to question the compatibility of Freemasonry with Christianity'.

Like many other Freemasons I am immensely grateful to the many clergy of all ranks and dignitaries who have gone out of their way to express encouragement and support in these circumstances; but I saw my task as being to see that brethren in my Province saw the matter in perspective, continued (as was their duty) to give support even to an officially unsympathetic church, continued to think out for themselves and in the light of all the facts how each of them saw the true relationship between religion and Freemasonry and between Church and Craft, and above all did not over-react but behaved with dignity and moderation.

MUCH HAS BEEN said and written in the course of the past three centuries about the relationship between Freemasonry and religion; it is something which is again in our minds today. Many of course think there is no problem. For those who think that there is, opinions vary between two extremes: that Freemasonry is totally incompatible with some religion, usually Christianity; or that it is itself a religion. I am sure that I do not have to explain to this audience that Freemasonry certainly is not a religion but a system of morality which requires every candidate to affirm before he can be admitted that he owes his existence as a human being to a Supernatural Power, and stipulates that each member will abide by the dictates and creeds of his own professed religion.

The dividing line between morality and religion is finely drawn, but I see nothing incompatible between religion and a code of morality which is based on the highest and most unselfish of ethics so long as that moral code is supportive of and subservient to the individual's religious beliefs. One of the strengths of Freemasonry is that the morality which it teaches is confined to the general ground, that is, to what is accepted as good by all religions which hold love for God and for our fellow men as the most desirable basis for a system of conduct and behaviour, as Christianity most certainly does.

The reason why Freemasonry is not a religion is basically because it has no religious dogma and so it does not proclaim that any particular revelation is right or wrong but only that in religious matters a Freemason should follow the teaching and practise the devotional methods of his particular creed. But we do have to realise that there will always be some to whom any moral teaching which is not learnt solely in the context of a particular religion or sect will be unacceptable. Yet in the world today there is an increasing awareness of the need for understanding and tolerance between different faiths, so it does seem odd that a similar tolerance should not be extended to a system which, though not itself a religion, requires its members to practise their religion and yet allows men of different faiths to meet together in love and amity, something of vital importance to the whole world. But be that as it may, the debate does tend to get over-heated and emotional and we should be careful to 'keep our cool' as the vernacular has it. One of the best ways of doing this is by thinking carefully and analytically about the issues so that we can answer any critic or enquirer with conviction, avoiding emotive words and phrases and always observing that dividing line between moral code and religious belief.

In considering how to explain our case we must be sure that we understand the difference between secrecy and privacy. The former is today looked upon with suspicion while the latter is prized as an unquestionable right. We are entitled to claim a proper privacy and we should make it clear that we do so. It is only when privacy is abused in order to protect wrong doing or anti-social intent that it becomes secrecy and we ought to be quite certain about that distinction and defend it. In doing so we have to show that our activities as Royal Arch Companions fall on the acceptable side of the boundary and cannot be classified as wrong or anti-social. To that extent therefore we must be prepared to explain the meaning of the Order.

The distinction is exemplified very clearly in our ritual. The Sojourners, not yet accepted as entitled to join in political decisions or even as legitimately qualified to work on the building, did not hesitate to disclose details of their claims to be accepted as colleagues but refused to utter the Ineffable Name even in the Council itself. We should similarly be ready to explain the ethos of our Order, that is its acceptance of the moral standards inculcated in the Craft, but must insist that such a code is considered only as part of our duty to our Creator and in the context of eternity. We can and should in my view claim the privilege of privacy for such matters as the details of the Sojourners' story and the signs and words of recognition in Craft and Royal Arch.

The Ineffable Name, the word on the circle, is sanctioned in the Holy Bible as having been divinely revealed, and this of course we can affirm openly; but it is by tradition not to be pronounced in Royal Arch meetings except with ceremonial reverence whatever may be the usage among non-masons. Why this should give offence to any Christian I am not able to understand, though there is of course great importance attached in many religions to any name of a deity, and in the Jewish and Christian traditions the use of certain names has been considered idolatrous. Whether you agree or disagree about that is not the point since all such beliefs are subjective. Earnest and sincere Christians who hold such views are entitled to know that there is a Name used in our ceremonies but we are entitled to stress that only the one Name is used and that not only is it sanctified by the Bible but it is treated with more reverence among us than it is sometimes accorded outside Freemasonry.

It is sometimes said in the context of discussion about the compatibility of Freemasonry and religion, particularly the Christian religion, that it is the Royal Arch which causes the most difficulty. I find this strange. To me, without the emphasis on the eternal which is the essence of the Royal Arch teaching Freemasonry would lose much of its relevance to our lives as mortals. The alleged problem seems to centre on the three letters and the word on the triangle, though the whole intent of these is to remind each Companion of the reverence due to the God he worships. Any mischief arises from mistaken and muddled work by early revisers of the ritual and by those who later, in an excess of misplaced zeal, allowed what is only a recognition word such as is found in many masonic degrees to be referred to as if it were a divine Name. I trust we are now rectifying that[3]. Unfortunately it has given our Christian critics the chance to misconstrue the letters and to claim that the second syllable of the recognition word is idolatrous, something which, if I have understood them correctly, can only be achieved by distorting its quantities. The argument seems to be based on two propositions. The first is that the word or its components or the letters are intended to comprise a name or names of God; insofar as this arises from our own mistakes, we must say so. The second is that they are idolatrous and this in plain English is nonsense; there is no reference to idols in them. To level accusations of heresy or blasphemy against God-fearing Anglicans who are serving their Church the better for the lessons they have learnt from Freemasonry is not the way forward and smacks of the methods of medieval times. We must always be ready to discuss and if necessary amend on good cause shown but we should be very careful about yielding to misguided and mistaken pressure.

These problems lead to the final point. The Royal Arch is commonly said to be the completion of the Third Degree of Craft masonry; and that, so far as it goes, is a true description because the Craft legend ends in loss, failure and death while that of the Royal Arch restores the loss, supplants failure with success and puts death in a true perspective by directing our attention to the prospect of eternity in which each Companion's religion will be his guide. The Royal

Arch demands that its members think about life in that context. The ritual should therefore help them to do so and not be in any way a hindrance. This is one important reason why we must support the efforts now being made to ensure that our ceremonies become easier to follow, and in particular to shorten the Third Lecture and purge it of inaccuracies and convoluted phraseology which not only strain our patience and credulity but also make it difficult to retain the interest of those we seek to instruct and guide.

All this is of course only a personal approach. But I hope it may help you to consider the important questions of why the Royal Arch is an integral part of Freemasonry, what our critics are saying about it, where they appear to have been misled or may have led themselves astray, and why the charges which are now being considered are important. We have much to do in the months that lie ahead and we shall emerge the stronger for it. Never lose sight of the fact that we bring men of different races and creeds together in peace, love and unity and that in doing so with some success we can with humility claim to be carrying out our duty to God, to our neighbours and to ourselves.

[1] *Freemasonry and Christianity, Are They Compatible?* Church House Publishing. ISBN 0 7151 3716 6.

[2] *Towards a Theology for Inter-Faith Dialogue.* Published for the Anglican Consultative Council by Church House Publishing 1984; second edition. ISBN 0 7151 5525 (In 'Final Reflections' [paras 81-85 of this Report] the authors describe the consensus of view which they have personally found as 'inclusivist with an exclusivist loyalty to Jesus Christ').

[3] On 8 February 1989 Supreme Grand Chapter resolved after a long and interesting debate that the word on the triangle and the letters should no longer appear on the pedestal and that all references to them should be removed from the ritual, largely on the ground of expediency. Those interested should study the official minutes.

13
THE CRITICS' CASE (1988)

By June 1988 the orchestrated hysteria about Freemasonry was dying down and it was time to take stock before returning to the discussion of the meaning of the Order. In particular, it was desirable to try to understand the genuine misgivings of serious critics and why we felt their fears to be misconceived. There was another reason for wishing to get 'on course' again: I was due to retire in two years and hoped before that to summarize my philosophy about the Order by putting forward a balanced and constructive view of what it should mean to be a Companion in the Royal Arch. In this light the criticisms and problems of the past few years, although they had been of use in forcing us to think objectively about Freemasonry, had been a distraction. It is always difficult to take an objective view in a matter where one is emotionally involved, and as most Freemasons enjoy their Freemasonry there was bound to be a degree of such involvement. But it was essential to lay as objective a foundation as possible if the task of the next two years was to be performed successfully.

Some of the quotations used in this address have already appeared in the Deanery Synod address but of course in a somewhat different context as that was delivered to a non-masonic audience.

WE ARE NOW emerging from one of those periods when the Christian churches feel it necessary to make pronouncements about Freemasonry. We cannot deny and never have denied their right to do so. Equally, they cannot deny our right to discuss and even to disagree with their conclusions. But what is necessary is that there should be a dialogue and that each party to that dialogue should be willing to listen, and not only to listen but to hear.

What then have we heard? I would suggest there are two things of importance. The first, and less obvious is that the churches in general, and the Church of England in particular, are consciously trying to redefine their attitude to non-Christian religions. The world appears a much smaller place now than it did in medieval times when so much of Christian theology was taking shape, and we live in a multi-faith community rather than in one which is exclusively Christian. This was briefly and unconvincingly referred to in the report of the Church of England working party[1]; but its development may well affect the light in which the churches will come to view Freemasonry. Three quotations, all from Church of England sources will I hope show you why.

First, you will recall the words of the Archbishop of York in the General Synod debate; and here I quote, 'We badly need good contexts in which people with different religious convictions can work together, without abandoning those convictions or without ignoring them. Freemasonry, as I understand it, has tried to provide such a context . . . I think the Craft needs to be commended for at least trying to solve an exceedingly difficult problem'.

Secondly, in a book called *We Believe in God* published recently with the approval of the Anglican bishops, you will find these words, 'We believe that the Christian revelation is true in many respects in which [that of other faiths] is false. But there is also much in Christian and other traditions which overlaps — enough to suggest that all are in touch in some degree with a single reality which, in these different idioms, is acknowledged and worshipped as God. They can become part of the resources of reason and experience which help to make explicit the doctrine of God implied in our own Scripture and tradition; and this should lead us to show openness and reverence towards the beliefs and practices of others'[2].

Lastly, I refer to a discussion document prepared for this year's Lambeth Conference of bishops of the world-wide Anglican Communion. It is called *Towards a Theology for Inter-Faith Dialogue* and one of its themes is that 'the Holy Spirit, present in the Church and in the lives of baptized Christians, is also active among those of other faiths and cultures'[3]. An example of this forms the very basis of the Royal Arch legend for, and here I am quoting from the *Book of Ezra*, '. . . the LORD stirred up the spirit of Cyrus king of Persian, that he made a proclamation . . . saying . . . . "The LORD God of Heaven . . . hath charged me to build him an house in Jerusalem" '[4]. Cyrus was of course the Persian conqueror of the Babylonian empire and neither he nor those he conquered were Jews or worshipped the God of the Jews; yet it was to him that the command was given and he recognized its origin. He not only listened; he also heard even across the barriers of religious differences.

As Freemasons we must recognize how difficult and potentially divisive these problems can become for Christians, and particularly for the Church of England in its tenure, not always an easy one, of the middle ground between the Roman Catholic and non-conformist traditions. Even if we feel hurt, as I know many of you do, because we believe that we have been unfairly criticized we must in these circumstances remain patient, understanding and receptive.

The second important thing I think we have heard is a concern that Freemasonry is straying from its role as a supporter of religious belief to become a religion in itself. I do not understand how it can be said that a system of morality which insists that each of its members must not only profess a religious belief before he is admitted to it as a member but continue to practise his religion after admission, can logically be said to be itself a religion. It was a favourite phrase of Dr Oliver's that Freemasonry is a 'humble handmaiden of religion' and that well expresses its supportive role. It is not and must never become, a religion.

Each of us knows of course that his own religion has core beliefs on which no compromise is possible and that anything which opposes such beliefs cannot be compatible with it. The mistake which it seems to me, in all humility, some of our critics make is to assume that we oppose a religion unless we require our members to adopt its tenets exclusively, which is self-evident nonsense. So far as Christianity is concerned let me quote again from the Lambeth discussion paper: 'What impels us [that is, Christians] to dialogue [that is, discussion with those of other faiths] is the belief that we are all created in the image of God, share a common humanity and all live in the presence of God'[5]. The paper goes on to emphasize that for a Christian this must always be within an exclusive loyalty to Christ as the Anointed of God. This inclusive yet exclusive position reflects very accurately the attitude of those Christian Freemasons with whom I have had the privilege of discussing the matter. We must nevertheless try to understand the difficulty felt by some Christians because we join in prayers which are not specifically and exclusively Christian, though it is difficult to see how there is to be any progress in inter-faith dialogue without inter-faith meetings for prayer.

Before going on to try to deduce what lessons we might learn from all this, I ought to refer to the difficulties which the General Synod report chose to see in respect of the Royal Arch. We were already dealing with certain points and we should bear in mind that the initiative was ours. That initiative is proceeding and we are about to debate the latest proposals of our own working party. The most important of them is that we should drop the word on the triangle from the ritual without any substitute. I think this is right; it has proved impossible to agree a substitute Royal Arch word and further delay must damage the Order[6]. The existing word has been compromised by having been mistakenly described as a name by well-meaning but possibly over-enthusiastic ritual re-writers; and even though the construction placed upon it by the Church of England report relies on untenable and to my mind unscholastic interpretation the damage is beyond redeeming. On the other hand I think that, having done our part, there is no need to enter into further discussion outside the Craft at this stage.

What then of the future? Theologians thrive on argument; it is the very marrow of theology, and Christian theologians have been arguing with one another for nearly two thousand years. The theological minefield is not a place for amateurs. It is by example that we must convince and the process will not be quick. Here a quotation from the letter which the Bishop of Peterborough sent to me on 17 July 1987 is in point. He wrote: '. . . . although I have never been a Mason I have always valued those men in my congregations across the years who found the craft to be a great blessing to them and saw no question of divided loyalty. They were among my best supports and I know that countless Vicars across the country who are not themselves members of the craft would say exactly the same'. It was a helpful and encouraging letter, and you will see how his views were formed by example. This encourages my belief that there is a way forward if we continue to conduct ourselves as we have heretofore, trying in both, and I stress this, in both faith and behaviour to set an example in our service to our churches and our communities, patiently explaining what Freemasonry is, and more importantly what it is not, while trying also to understand the problems others may think they see. We may fairly point out too that archbishops, bishops, priests and ministers of many denominations have been happy to acknowledge themselves openly as Freemasons. Remember that we have nothing of which to be ashamed. Brotherly love, relief and truth are still our lodestars; respect for each man's religion is for us a basic principle; and the grand design of being happy and more importantly of communicating happiness is one of our most challenging aims. In words of the ritual which remind the Christians among us of the teachings of Christ Himself, and particularly of His parable of the talents, we must 'exert those talents wherewith God has blessed us, as well to His glory as the welfare of our fellow-creatures'. When the final tally comes to be reckoned, such matters must surely appear on the credit side of the ledger for anyone who has lived by them and by the tenets of his religion.

---

[1] See chapter 1, note 11, and Appendix B.
[2] See chapter 1, note 13, This passage is on pp 13-14.
[3] Para 61. Published by Church House Publishing, ISBN 0 7151 5525 3.
[4] Ezra, 1: 1-2. Authorised Version.
[5] Para 63.
[6] The word has been removed from the ritual; see chapter 12, note 3.

14
'BROTHERLY LOVE, RELIEF ...' (1989)

The two final addresses were an attempt to sum up as briefly as possible a philosophy of the Royal Arch. The approach to such a matter is bound to be highly individual, but to state one's own thinking may help readers to form their own views; when delivered it was not, and is not now, intended to be didactic. A particular problem arose as a result of revisions of the ritual of which most but not all Companions approved; this had been in progress before the Churches (and more sensationally the press) began 'investigations' which sometimes seemed emotional if not hysterical and in some cases could hardly be praised for accuracy. But the basic principles of Freemasonry remain unchanged and so the question arises, 'is Freemasonry, which can be seen as a child of the past, relevant to the world of today as we approach the twenty-first century?' That question had to be answered for the Craft in general before one could consider the meaning and relevance of the Royal Arch.

Trying to help Companions of my Province to see the problems of the past few years in perspective had somewhat shortened the time for such discussion; but on the other hand there had been one unexpected and positive result of all the fuss: it had made the task of revising the ritual much easier than it might otherwise have been. The last previous occasion on which it had been revised officially was in 1834/5 when a committee containing a strong representation of Anglican priests had been appointed for the purpose by HRH the Duke of Sussex, Grand Master; without the spur provided by the Churches in particular the question of revision might well have dragged on for some time. So from the point of view of the Craft, and particularly of the Royal Arch, there had been some compensation for the hurt which had undoubtedly been caused to the feelings of the many God-fearing Freemasons. Now there were two years left and the pressure was on me; the 1989 address was therefore the first of two which looked at these questions of meaning and relevance.

WHEN WE ARE asked 'What is Freemasonry?' the answer that trips most glibly off the tongue is 'a system of morality, veiled in allegory and illustrated by symbols'. Lately we have probably been anxious to stress that it is concerned with morality and neither is nor claims to be a religion; and we tend to be rather proud about the allegory and symbols even though today we pay far too little attention to them. But what is this system? What, so to speak, holds our teaching together and makes it a system? These are not easy questions to answer, yet we must be prepared to answer them if we are to remain credible. After all, it is we who define it as a 'system' and enquirers might rightly expect us to justify our claim, while our critics may with justice mock if we cannot do so.

Morality itself is not easy to define; we soon find that even those we respect may differ from each other about detailed moral issues. And a very small amount of research will show you that what is generally regarded as moral by any community changes over the years. Thus Christ modified the codes of Moses; and thus today divorce no longer carries, for the majority of the population, the stigma that attached to it in the first quarter of this century. So too we find modern theologians criticizing the Craft for practices which their predecessors considered to accord with Christian principles. We can multiply examples, but we all know how much and how rapidly customs and manners have changed and are changing today. Is it now time for us to change the basis of our system?

The answer will depend on whether Freemasonry postulates standards which are adequate and appropriate for the world today. It is a fast changing world, but there are two unchanging constants for mankind, the need to worship the Divine Creator the satisfaction of which is one of the greatest functions of religion, and the need to establish standards which will allow us to live together in the Creator's world in peace, love and harmony, as individuals, as families, as communities, as nations, as a world, which is the great function of morality. To this second function Freemasonry contributes because the level of behaviour which we expect from brethren in their dealings with their fellow creatures in this world is based on those virtues which the history of every religion, philosophy or civilization worthy of the name proves to be the foundation of happiness and goodwill. We summarize them as Brotherly Love, Relief (which is charity, or as I prefer to call, compassion) and Truth (which is moral behaviour, exerting those talents wherewith God has blessed us as well to His glory as the welfare of our fellow creatures as the ritual puts it). Those three provide the basis of the system of morality which we profess and teach. We accept that it is from God that our talents derive and that we must account to God for the use which we make of them. This is a basic teaching of the Holy Royal Arch, which our critics seem so determined to misunderstand. We must constantly make it clear that we require every Freemason to practise the religion he professes and to pay due obedience to the laws of the State in which he resides. 'Due obedience', not blind obedience, so that a Freemason is expected not to act in a manner contrary to the dictates of his religion, the feelings of his heart, or the proper interests of those who in any sense depend upon him.

These points are important because some of our critics seem to believe that by our teaching we are trying to form or even alter a brother's religious beliefs and do not seem to realize, or perhaps even do not want to realize, that we require every brother to view that teaching in the context of the beliefs and teachings of his own religion. We appreciate that a critic may sincerely believe that only a strict conformity to the religious tenets he accepts, which are often narrow in their scope, can ensure the well-being of the individual souls of mankind, and of course we respect such sincerity. But Freemasonry encourages us to meet together in brotherly love in spite of differences of creed and dogma; that is surely something which men of goodwill everywhere could be expected to welcome in this divided world, something which made it possible for me not so long ago to sit in amity and friendship at lunch with the Inspector General of the Ancient and Accepted Rite for Zimbabwe on my left and the Grand Superintendent for Transvaal on my right; or which recently allowed the Grand Lodge of Israel to elect as its Grand Master an Arab Christian. Such things are symbolic of standards which, while respecting the earnestly held beliefs of our critics, we must maintain.

A system of morality will not be complete unless it takes account of darker days, times of sorrow, or moments when we are disappointed in our hopes or dismayed by the actions or neglect of others or feel that we have not lived up to our own standards. The alternate black and white tesserae on the floor of the Lodge room remind us that the days of our earthly pilgrimage will not all be joyful. But they remind us too that all is not gloom and even perhaps that we must be prepared to pass through the darkness if we are ever to approach the perfection for which each of us strives within the context of his beliefs. If the Sojourners had not been ready to dare the perils of the unknown by venturing into the vault which they had uncovered they would never have found the prize that lay there.

But look a little deeper into this story of the Sojourners, for it has more to tell us. Three men had come home from exile and were so glad to be received and welcomed that they did not mind accepting any task, however menial, which could contribute to the common enterprise of rebuilding the House of God. Not all of us can be priests or rulers or even expect to attain the position which we feel would enable us to serve our fellow men best. The Sojourners understood why they could not be employed on more skilled or prestigious work, and knew that attainment of the objective demanded that everyone should perform his allotted task, however, lowly, to the limit of his ability. But neither were they foolhardy; only one was to venture, the others were to be at hand to see that he could be hauled to safety when the need arose. In a sense their task was easier than ours because if their companion was in peril his danger would at once be known to them; we in our everyday lives cannot always tell when a Companion is miserable or depressed because convention demands that he does not upset us by disturbing our complacency. But we are proud to be called Companions and as Companions it is our duty to see his need, even though it be unspoken, and to be at hand to help him. It will help us to achieve this if we obey the injunction to 'communicate happiness' because by doing so we become more sensitive to the needs of others.

But Brotherly Love does not mean love for the Brethren only. No-one can expect to avoid dark days and it is our duty as Freemasons to help our fellow mortals through them by ensuring that our demeanour is such that anyone, whether or not a member of the Craft, may know that a Freemason will try to provide comfort for 'the burdened heart', and that the distressed may indeed readily 'prefer their suit' to him. The Samaritans were regarded as heretics by orthodox Jews but Christ, himself a Jew, gave us the parable of the Good Samaritan. The option of passing by on the other side is not open to a Freemason. 'Relief' or compassion as I have called it, neither begins nor ends with your cheque book.

You may wonder why I have laboured this point in the context of our 'system of morality'. It is because sympathy, which literally means 'feeling with' or 'feeling for', is the common denominator in each of the moral virtues in which we sum up our system; love, compassion and moral behaviour. It is the factor which down the ages has always brought out the best in humanity, and one which the world needs today more than ever before as the frontiers of knowledge advance, as physical frontiers shrink and man struggles towards an internationalism he does not yet seem ready to accept, and as the rewards and dangers of the future confront us so starkly. Yes, Companions, we do have a system of morality; and yes, it is adequate for today as it has been for times past and will be for times yet to come. Every Freemason can without difficulty apply its principles within the context of the teachings of his religion. We have no reason to change it and every reason to be proud of it.

15
'. . . AND TRUTH' (1990)

If the Craft has a place and relevance in the modern world, then surely the same should apply to the Supreme Order of the Holy Royal Arch. But does it? More importantly, is 'Brotherly Love, Relief and Truth' an adequate definition of the objects of an Order whose members are taught to contemplate existence within a context of eternity? And does this concentration on things eternal impinge in any way on the territory of religion? The final address had to cover a great deal of ground but was a humble attempt to set these problems in perspective and to encourage Companions of the Order to find their own answers in the light of whatever religion each might profess.

Preparing these addresses for the printer I have been wondering whether one point has been sufficiently stressed in them; that Freemasonry does not imply, as one correspondent has suggested to me, that 'morality should seek religion merely to identify and support moral principles'. In fact the reverse is the case; for a man to become a Freemason he must have a religious belief and for him that must be paramount. So a Christian Freemason, believing he is saved by Grace, will regard Freemasonry as helping him to carry out the second commandment given by Christ, to love his neighbour as himself. Being in the company of other men who have also confessed a belief in a Supreme Being may help him to stand firm in his religious belief (as has been my own experience) and thus assist him to observe the first commandment; the whole thrust of masonic teaching is that the practice of his religion is the most important thing in a man's life. I feel as I write these words that I have still not adequately explained something that is very important to me; Dr Oliver put it succinctly when he wrote the words quoted in another address 'morality is not the groundwork but the result and fruit of religion'. The strength of the masonic code of morality in this connection is that it is based on virtues acknowledged as such by all the great religions and insists that for every man his religion is supreme.

THE PLEASANT TASK of ruling this Royal Arch Province for twelve years has made me think hard about the place of the Order in Freemasonry, its relevance to the world in which we live and to the hereafter to which we hope to attain, and each year at our Annual Convocation I have tried in all humility to encourage you too to think about these things. It has been a kind of pilgrim's progress, wandering hither and thither but advancing hopefully towards a glimpsed but as yet unseen goal; and always you have encouraged and helped me so that we have journeyed together. Now, on the last occasion on which I shall be privileged to address you as your Grand Superintendent, it is time to see what progress we have made.

Let me start with the relationship of our Order to the Craft. We say that the Royal Arch is the completion of the Third Degree, but why is that so? The glib answer is that it concerns the finding of that which was lost, but though in another Order we can learn more about the masonic tradition of a secret vault and its contents[1] the legend of the Royal Arch only mentions a few items, a veiled column, a plate of gold bearing the Ineffable Name of God as it was revealed to Moses, and the earliest books of the Bible, lost secrets perhaps, but not the signs the loss of which is part of the Craft legend. The Royal Arch signs are indeed disclosed later in the ceremony and take the place of the five points of fellowship in which the Master Mason is instructed and which, being Craft signs, are concerned with our relationships with one another; the Royal Arch signs concern our relationship with our Creator, and in that difference you have an epitome of the most important contrast between the two Orders.

One of the Royal Arch signs has a particular relevance in this connection. If you think about the signs of the three Craft degrees you will realize that they relate only to this transitory life, and those of you who are Installed Masters will perceive that this is also true of what was revealed to you at your Installation. But there is a Craft sign which transcends this and calls our attention to the eternity in which our lives are set and to which it is the purpose of the Royal Arch to direct our thoughts. The peculiar nature of this sign is not explained in the ritual yet it is used more frequently than any other and is an accompaniment to prayer. But have you ever realized that it is not a complete sign? It is completed in the Royal Arch as the R or H sign whereby we adopt an attitude of prayer but at the same time acknowledge the majesty and glory of the Creator, qualities which our ancestors called awe and which we call reverence. This is yet another example of the way in which the Holy Royal Arch turns the challenging light of eternity on to the earthbound teachings of the Craft. Let me remind you of others to which I have from time to time drawn your attention.

In the Third Degree we are told that five Fellow Crafts opened the ground and found a dead body; in the Royal Arch three Sojourners opened the vault and found the Ineffable Name[2]. Again, the first things that a candidate sees in the ceremony of Initiation are the three great lights that will guide him on his journey through life; in the Exaltation ceremony the first thing the candidate sees is an emblematical representation of that journey as a pilgrimage towards eternity, something to which I drew your attention in 1981[3] and something which is emblematically depicted on your Grand Chapter certificate in contrast to the earthly virtues depicted in that of the Craft.

The Craft legend ends in loss, despair and death, hardly an inspiring or satisfactory conclusion for what is described as 'a system of morality'. The Holy Royal Arch completes the picture by showing us that loss, death and despair do not have the final word; in a phrase you will have heard me use before, it puts the teaching of the Craft into the frame or context of eternity; and it is after all eternity with which we should be primarily concerned as we travel through this transitory life to the time when we must give an account of the way in which we have used the talents bestowed on us.

Over the past three years events had led me to ask you to consider not only our relationship to the Craft but to whatever religion each of us may profess, and particularly to Christianity; and in 1989[4] I tried to examine our claim that Freemasonry is a system of morality and to see how that morality stood in relation to religion. This led to a discussion of our basic tenets, Brotherly Love, Relief and Truth — or as I preferred to phrase them, Love, Compassion and Morality, all summed up in the word Sympathy. That was adequate for the teaching of the Craft, but now I want to take the argument further in the light of what I have just said about the relationship between Craft and Chapter.

While the aspect of Truth with which we are concerned in the Craft relates to standards of moral behaviour, in the context of eternity Truth is more than morality; it is the basis of our existence, the answer to the riddle of our existence. Francis Bacon, in a famous essay, said that Pilate was jesting when he asked 'What is truth?' and 'would not stay for an answer'. With deference to a great scholar, I think Pilate put that question in despair, knowing how prone every human being is to claim that only his or her beliefs are true and how impossible it therefore was, as it still is for that matter, for any mortal judge to define truth by process of logical thought. For in fact Truth has two aspects; one is the standard by which we should live our lives in relation to one another and the second and more important is the ultimate reality which we cannot prove by logic but can only know by Faith. The first is the concern of morality, the second is the essence of religious belief, even though each religion, even each sect of the same religion, may approach it differently.

I want to stress this because otherwise it might be claimed that our system of morality could be agnostic; it is the inclusion of Truth in its widest sense that proves the contrary, so that a man cannot become a Freemason unless he believes that the universe and everyone and everything in it was divinely created; and as a Freemason he is expected to retain and nourish that belief by the practice of his religion.

But we must not be misled into thinking that therefore Freemasonry is a substitute for religion. We have already seen that in the Holy Royal Arch the thoughts of each Companion are directed to examine the moral lessons of the Craft in the light of eternal truths and of the account he must one day give of his life on earth — matters which every religion worthy of the name requires its adherents to consider. This is the true completion of the teaching of the Craft, and this I think is what Laurence Dermott, a great Grand Secretary of the eighteenth century, meant when he called the Order 'the root, heart and marrow of Freemasonry'. Brotherly Love, Relief and Truth (love, compassion and morality) are indeed the great principles on which the Craft rests, but Companions of this Order will recognize that Truth is more than morality, and is in fact the ancient quality of awe with its implications of discipline and obedience and for which our tamer modern term is 'reverence'. So for us, as Companions, I would read this triad as 'Love, Compassion and Reverence' — a reverence which is to be sought by each of us in the teachings of his own religion. Can it really be claimed by anyone that this is not compatible with his religion? Such a claim would make a mockery of an attempt at an interfaith theology, something about which I spoke with diffidence in my address to you in 1988[5].

Companions, in addressing you in these terms I am obeying a compulsion to summarize something which I feel deeply, a personal view of the Royal Arch which for me gives the whole structure of Freemasonry a real meaning as a code of conduct; and I hope that it may help you to appreciate this Order and to see attacks on Freemasonry, however motivated, in perspective. Each of us must think these things through for himself and all of us are still learning. For me, Freemasonry teaches men to care for others and to adopt high standards for themselves, and without the Chapter the Craft would not be complete; nor could I remain a Freemason unless I saw the Craft as subordinate to my religion and as a code of conduct in harmony with that religion.

I make no apology for the serious nature of this final address but take my leave with thanks to you all for your support, your kindness, and — in a word that says it all — your companionship during the years in which I have been privileged to hold this office of Grand Superintendent; and once again I say to you, as I have so often said before 'Enjoy your Masonry', but this time I add 'Think on these things, fare you well and God be with you all'.

[1] Order of Royal and Select Masters ('Cryptic' Masonry).
[2] See chapter 5.
[3] See chapter 6.
[4] See chapter 14.
[5] See chapter 13.

16
FROM BABYLON, MOST EXCELLENT

The earlier part of this book has been concerned with the origin and ethos of the Order of the Holy Royal Arch but there is a problem which sometimes puzzles Companions, particularly in these days when biblical knowledge is not widespread, the problem of the setting in which the events of the degree legend are put.

These events are separated from those of the Craft legend by some 500 years, the time scale which separates us from the earliest Tudors and the battle of Bosworth. Ten of the twelve tribes had disappeared, absorbed by their conquerors; Chaldeans and Babylonians had come on to the scene; and the legend of the degree begins with the appearance of the Persians as the dominant power in the area and the ending of the Babylonian captivity by Cyrus. How did all this happen? What were the forces that led to the downfall of Israel and then of Judah? Why was it so difficult to build the second Temple? What is the relevance of the Principals and Scribes who are mentioned in the Royal Arch? Only a knowledge of the historical background can provide the answers to these and other similar questions. And when we have the answers, what then? How did the legend arise? What does it mean to us today?

Inevitably research brings to light historical anomalies and sometimes these may challenge credibility. This is not a phenomenon peculiar to Freemasonry; the tools available to researchers today have thrown doubt on many legends which our ancestors regarded as established fact and latterly even biblical history has been challenged on various grounds. We have to keep firmly in mind that what matters in the context of morality is the lesson to be learnt from the story as it is told; few today believe the tale of Adam and Eve in the Garden of Eden to be a record of historical fact, but as allegorical teaching it can still be of value. What is essential in the Royal Arch is to understand the message which the ritual seeks to convey.

Because this talk is self-contained there is inevitably some repetition of points already made; but so that it can if desired be given as a lecture I have left it unaltered. It will, in the hands of a competent speaker, take about 35 minutes to deliver and I have found it advantageous to photograph the sketch map which accompanies it and distribute copies before the lecture starts.

'STRANGERS, WHENCE come you?' 'From Babylon, Most Excellent'. We are all familiar with these words as a prelude to one of the loveliest pieces of our ritual, too familiar perhaps, because we do not give them much thought, Yet they are worth thinking about and if spoken in the circumstances in which they are supposedly set they would have been as emotive as today's 'from a concentration camp'.

So what was the background to the story? What sort of place was Babylon? Who were the Chaldeans who lived there and how did it come to be the capital of the Persian king? Why was the first Temple destroyed? How did the Jewish people fare in captivity, and what sort of captivity was it? Why is the legend of the Sojourners important? And why is the Royal Arch essential to Freemasonry? All those questions are implicit in that brief colloquy, and this is an attempt to discuss them.

First we must establish when and where relevant events took place; in other words, we must refresh our knowledge of geography and history. Take geography first. The countries and peoples involved have changed over the centuries, acquiring new names and identities; so unless we first define areas and races the story may confuse rather than assist. I shall use the old terms Palestine, Asia Minor, Mesopotamia, Syria and Persia to describe the areas which concern us. Palestine will mean that part of the land at the eastern end of the Mediterranean Sea which lies west of the river Jordan; Asia Minor will be the eastern part of modern Turkey; Mesopotamia, the area through which the two rivers, Tigris and Euphrates flow south-eastwards towards the Persian Gulf, that is broadly the northern part of today's Iraq; Syria will mean the area between all those, that is modern Libya and Syria; and the area east of Mesopotamia, towards Afghanistan and India will be Persia, today's Iran. Of all these lands the most fertile and desirable were Palestine and Mesopotamia; much of the rest was either desert or mountainous.

These are not the only territories that figure in the story. There was ever and always Egypt, the country of the Nile valley, rich, highly civilized and jealous of its power and influence, linked to Palestine by the peninsular of Sinai across which the considerable landborne trade between Asia and Africa had to pass. Yet in spite of its advantages

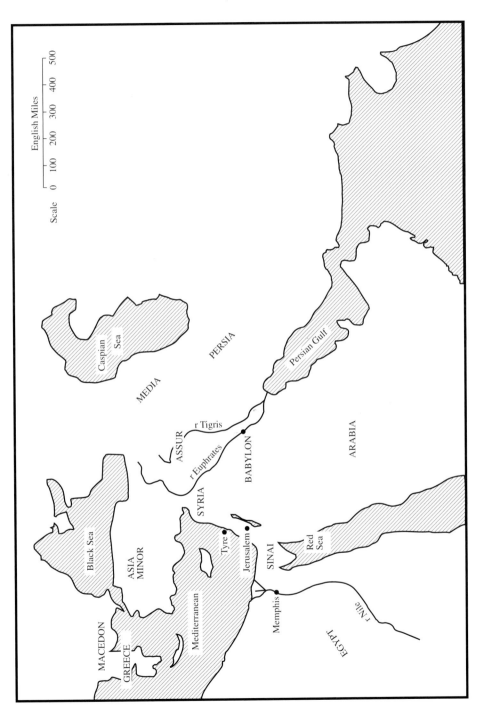

Egypt was not always strong; its system of government was central-
ized, and if the Pharaoh was weak the country was weak. In view of
the intensive inbreeding in the royal families it is not surprising that
the country's influence varied, but its increasing periods of weakness
gave more virile powers the opportunity to grow.

Many races dwelt in the area; the most important for our purpose
were the Jews, Assyrians, Chaldeans, Persians, and Medes.

Taking the Jews first, they had occupied a large part of Palestine on
their exodus from Egypt but they never held it all even at the height of
their power under David and his son Solomon. After the death of
Solomon in about 930 BC they split into two nations, Judah in the
south with two tribes and Israel in the north with ten; these two were
soon at war with each other. The northern kingdom was the larger, the
southern comprising only the small area allotted to the tribes of Judah
and Benjamin, though this smaller area included Jerusalem, the city
David developed as his capital and where the Temple was founded
that David had planned and Solomon had built. It is important to
remember that until the time of the Babylonian captivity the Jews had
no system of synagogues or places of worship throughout the land;
the place for worship was the Temple at Jerusalem, the House of God,
and it was the duty of every Jew to go there to worship and sacrifice
or make an offering whenever the law called for such action. It has to
be recorded that a great many of them from time to time worshipped
local gods, they and their rulers had constantly to be reminded by the
prophets — whose role we must consider later — of their duty to God
Who had brought the Children of Israel out of Egyptian captivity into
'a land flowing with milk and honey' as the Bible describes it.

But the richness of that land made it attractive to others; and it lay
between the Egyptians who had once possessed it and powerful forces
beginning to develop to the east. Babylonia was a loose collection of
three provinces which together occupied the land at the head of the
Persian Gulf, on the lower reaches of the rivers Tigris and Euphrates
in the southern part of Mesopotamia. Its capital was Babylon on the
lower Euphrates. In the land between the upper reaches of those
rivers, roughly between Asia Minor and Persia, was the state of Assur
which had been over the centuries in conflict with the kings of Babylonia. The Assyrians eventually took Babylon and then in 732 BC
captured Damascus in Syria, thereby exposing the northern Jewish
kingdom of Israel to their attacks. Samaria, the capital of that kingdom, fell to them in 722 BC, about 200 years after the death of
Solomon; the Jews of the northern kingdom were carried off to the
east by their captors and soon lost their identity; the ten tribes in fact
simply disappeared from history. The charming book of Tobit in the

Apocrypha gives us a vivid picture of a Jewish way of life crumbling under Assyrian influence.

At its greatest extent the Assyrian empire included Egypt, Syria, most of Palestine and the south-east part of Asia minor, and stretched to the Persian Gulf in the south; but Judah managed to maintain a precarious and nominally independent existence, a tribute to the strategic genius of David in choosing it as his capital and to the faith of the Jews in their destiny as the Chosen People of God, even though they vacillated in their worship from time to time. The temple, the religious focal point of the Jewish faith, remained as a solid testimony to their status as His people, and was a centre of encouragement and resistance to outside influences even though in the course of the centuries many of its original splendours were seized by hostile armies or paid away as tribute to neighbouring powers. But its role as a central rallying point was undoubtedly one of the reasons why it was so utterly destroyed later.

The Assyrian empire lasted until about 600 BC. It fell to a new dynasty of Chaldeans who had seized the throne of Babylonia. Chaldea was the area round the mouths of the Euphrates and Tigris, an agriculturally rich part of Babylonia. The Chaldeans overthrew the Assyrians with the help of the Medes, a race established in Persia who, having recently themselves thrown off the yoke of the Assyrians, were now glad to help destroy the empire. The Chaldeans established themselves in Babylon and the zenith of their power was under Nebuchadnezzar the Great who reigned just after the fall of Assyria, in achieving which he had taken a prominent part. It was by his order that Jerusalem and the Temple were destroyed. Jehoiachin, king of Judah, surrendered the city to him on 16 March 597 BC, and Nebuchadnezzar took him and many leading citizens to Babylon as captives, along with most of the remaining treasures. When the puppet king he had left behind in Jerusalem, Zedekiah, rebelled nine years later the Assyrians again invaded and after a siege which lasted 18 months and left the people starving and weak, he took the city, sacked and burnt it and the Temple and left the devastated ruins to wind and weather.

To the east of Babylon the Medes had continued to prosper. They were a people whose history became inextricably linked with that of the Persians. Some 12 years after Nebuchadnezzar died the Persian Cyrus became king of the Medes by overthrowing his father-in-law, the Median ruler. Cyrus was ambitious and he soon marched against Babylon, which he captured without opposition in 539 BC; so you will see that the Chaldean empire which plays such an important part in our legend lasted less than 100 years. Cyrus and his successors extended their empire eastward to India and westward into Europe. In the south their boundary became approximately the northern border of modern Arabia. Egypt and much of the southern shore of the eastern Mediterranean also came under their rule.

There are now two other races to mention. First the Greeks, a people of city states often indulging in vicious internecine warfare with each other; warfare which ultimately destroyed them. They established a number of colonial outposts along the coasts of Asia Minor and on many of the islands at the western end of the Mediterranean. They were a maritime race — a fact which was to enable them, about 60 years after the fall of Babylon, to halt the westward spread of the Persian empire at the battle of Salamis in 480 BC. Ten years before, they had defeated the Persians by land at the battle of Marathon and of these two battles it really can be said that they changed the course of history for they not only allowed the growth of the northern Greek state of Macedon but also gave the emergent city of Rome in the west time to establish itself as a dominant power. Though considered by the southern Greeks to be almost barbarians, the rudest term in the vocabulary of early west European civilization, the Macedonians were a martial race, and as the city states of mainland Greece decayed, exhausted by their feuds and constant wars, the power of Macedon grew. About a century and a half after the battle of Salamis, under a young military genius who became known to history as Alexander the Great, it overthrew the Persians and briefly established its rule all over the countries we have been considering.

The other race was the Phoenicians who traded by sea over the whole Mediterranean and even beyond, establishing a number of trading posts on the mainland, of which one of the most famous was Hiram's city of Tyre, a rich and powerful port which withstood all invaders until Alexander took and sacked it in the course of his eastward progress.

These two races, Greeks and Phoenicians, in effect set bounds to the spread of the Persian empire by the exercise of sea-power. In doing so they paved the way for the Macedonian conquest and the spread of Greek influences over the whole of what we now call the Middle East. Even the Jews felt their influence though in the end they rejected it and reverted to their old religion, a characteristic that had been much to the fore in the Babylonian captivity and which accounts for the energy and determination with which they set about re-establishing their culture and religion at the end of that captivity.

It will be seen that in these areas changes of power tended to be cataclysmic rather than gradual, but until Nebuchadnezzar sacked Jerusalem its Jewish inhabitants had managed to retain their ancient religion and customs, their essential separateness, and the Temple had remained a focus for their occasional turbulent outbursts of independence even though their kings paid tribute to their powerful neighbours. In times of stress the Temple was a reminder to them that the House of their God was in Jerusalem and that they were His people and under His protection; unfortunately they did not always remember to worship Him and were continually having to be reminded that He might withdraw His protection if they did not behave in accordance with His commandments.

The destruction of the Temple by Nebuchadnezzar was intended to erase forever the Jewish awareness of the nationhood of their race and to destroy their God. But the Chaldeans never understood that the God of the Jewish race was not a physical idol like their Chaldean gods and the destruction of the city and Temple had the very opposite effect to that which had been intended, for faced with the ultimate calamity the Jews of Judah did not allow themselves to be absorbed into the civilization of their captors but clung the more steadfastly to their essential separateness. Their intellectual, administrative and financial abilities were such as the administration of a large empire required, and on the whole they seem to have prospered. 'By the waters of Babylon we sat down and wept when we remembered thee, O Sion' the poet lamented, but they had the assurance of the prophet Jeremiah that after 70 years their captivity would end and they accepted this as the will of God. During that captivity they recalled their history and traditions and wrote them down. Many of the books of the Bible took the form in which we know them at that time. Unlike the Jews of the former northern kingdom, a significant proportion of them never forgot the city and the Temple and the older generation kept the memories and traditions alive for their children; in this they were aided and encouraged by the prophets in Babylon and Judah.

These prophets were a phenomenon peculiar to the Jews. Other races had their own particular magic men and doomsters who usually seem to have made a good living out of their profession. The prophets were looked upon as a race set apart. They were believed to be inspired by God Whose will they declared to men. In doing this a prophet would frequently reproach the people and their rulers and convey unsavoury truths to them. When later the state became a monarchy this was a somewhat hazardous occupation and prophets sometimes suffered exile, imprisonment or death as the penalty for daring to critizise an absolute monarch. Nevertheless they were powerful; they represented in a very real way the conscience of the people, and often it was a somewhat guilty conscience. They took kings,

priests and people to task unmercifully for their failings and in doing
so preserved the memory of the old traditions of history and of worship which otherwise might have died out. They were held in reverence and awe, and were often feared, as we can see from the question
put to Samuel when he arrived at Jesse's house to anoint David. The
first thought on seeing the prophet approaching was to ask, 'Comest
thou peaceably?' They were astute politicians and dispassionate
observers; they read the signs of their times, and when the decadence
of the people and their rulers inevitably brought about the calamities
they had foretold, their prestige was thereby enhanced. The triple con-
junction of the secular, priestly and prophetical dispensations
reflected in the Royal Arch bears witness to their importance.

In fact, Judah was so small and physically insignificant in the historical context of the time, something we tend to forget because of the
importance of the Bible in our civilization, and its rulers were so often
given to luxury and ease, not to mention conspiracy, that the prophets
could not lose. But it is important to realize the stabilizing influence
they had and the effect of their constant reiteration of the old beliefs
as reminding the Jews of the traditions of their race and of their
unique position as the 'chosen people' even in times of adversity. The
knowledge that a prophet had foretold the end of the Babylonian captivity and promised a return to Jerusalem meant that the Jews in
Babylon regarded themselves as exiles, mere sojourners, and that in
spite of the might of their captors and of the constant efforts made to
persuade them to abandon their faith, they looked forward to their
return home in the sure knowledge that it would happen. So when
Babylon fell as the time forecast for the ending of their exile drew
near, they would be greatly encouraged and when they discovered that
Cyrus was minded to reverse the depopulating policies of his predecessors, they saw an opportunity which they hastened to exploit.

It will be as well now to attempt some description of Babylon in
the time of Nebuchadnezzar the Great since it was the centre of the
environment in which the tribes of Judah and Benjamin lived for
some 60 years, and its luxury, strength and splendour must inevitably
have made an impression upon them. It was a very highly civilized
city, well laid out and wealthy to a degree that defies the imagination.
Its walls were extensive and are said by some to have been over 40
miles long though many modern archaeologists doubt this. They were
surrounded by a moat filled with running water. The Greek historian
Herodotus recorded that the walls were some 200 cubits high and 50
broad, and as the modern equivalent for the cubit is usually considered to be 45 centimetres or 17.5 inches you will see that if he was not
exaggerating (he was rather prone to exaggeration) they were nearly

90 metres or 300 feet in height and over 70 feet wide. Mary Reynaud in her very readable book *The Nature of Alexander* describes them in fact as 400 feet high and 180 feet thick. Certainly they were massive, so much so that the top was broad enough to allow a four horse chariot to turn in its width.

Much of the city which the captive Jews would see had been rebuilt by Nebuchadnezzar. There were many fine streets and some houses were 3 or 4 storeys high. It straddled the river Euphrates across which there were a number of bridges. The main street, the great processional way, was dedicated to the principal god of the Chaldeans, Marduk or Bel, and led to his great temple in which the bulk of the treasures and sacred vessels from the Temple at Jerusalem were stored. According to a story recorded in the book of Daniel in the Bible, it was the use of some of these vessels for drinking at a feast given by a later Chaldean king, Belshazzar, that occasioned the episode which has given us the phrase 'the writing on the wall'.

Such then was the greatest city of the empire which Cyrus the Persian acquired without even a siege in 539 BC. It would seem that many of the Jews had been living there, and some such as Daniel had acquired high office; we are told that under the Persians Zerubbabel was an officer of the king's bodyguard and later that Nehemiah was cup-bearer to the king. They had from time to time been subjected to religious persecution which gave rise to such stories as that of Daniel in the lion's den; and even after the return to Jerusalem of the first Jewish party the Book of Esther relates that one Haman persuaded the king to issue an edict for the slaughter on a given date of all the Jews in the empire and was only thwarted by the courageous intervention of Queen Esther, herself a Jewess. Haman ended up hanging on the tall gibbet he had built for the execution of Esther's father and so gave us the saying 'hanged as high as Haman'.

The Persians, though they could be cruel, were in general much less harshly disposed towards captive peoples than the Assyrians and were tolerant in matters of religious differences. Cyrus and his successors were in any case compelled by political considerations to reckon with the religions of their subject peoples and skilfully made use of this necessity to help hold their empire together and to man its outposts.

The Jews had seen the fulfilment of the prophecy that foretold the fall of Babylon and though it had not been destroyed as a city the Chaldean rule had been ended, and they seem pragmatically to have set about winning favour with the new regime and obtaining permission to return and rebuild the Temple. From the point of view of Cyrus there was no reason to detain them in restive sojourn in

Babylon where they could threaten his peace, while if packed off to Jerusalem they would have to defend the western borders of his new empire against the ever-watchful jealousy of Egypt. About a year after the capture of Babylon he allowed them to go. The first party seem to have left in about 538 BC, some 60 years after the capture of Jerusalem and 50 after the final destruction of Solomon's Temple.

I have painted all this with a very broad brush but now we come to the point where detail must be more prominent, and I emphasize that almost all the dates are disputed, particularly those relating to Nehemiah; but I do not want to bore you with the quarrels of the experts so will take a somewhat empiric approach and do my best on what seems to be the balance of probabilities.

Ezra, writing some 80 years later, says that about fifty thousand people returned to Jerusalem in the first party with 736 horses, 245 mules, 435 camels and 6720 asses; quite a caravan. At the end of it (and Ezra says that his later party, who were hurrying, took four months to travel the same distance) their troubles were far from over. They were more than 500 miles from Babylon, and the firman, the imperial decree authorizing their return and the rebuilding of the Temple, though granted by Cyrus, was not welcomed by the local rulers who would in any case be in a traumatic state of nerves in the aftermath of the overthrow of the seemingly invincible empire, and very careful not to wrongfoot themselves. The rebuilding of the Temple and of the city walls, with all its implications of Jewish nationalism and pride, would be a matter of considerable concern to them and quite contrary not only to established policy but also to local interests. Not unnaturally they forced a stoppage of the work and referred back to Babylon.

The firman of Cyrus had been granted to Sheshbazzar who was probably the son of Jehoiachin, king of Judah, and uncle of Zerubbabel; we know little of him and he does not play any prominent part in the scripture stories; presumably he died before the work could really be started. But Joshua and Zerubbabel had at once set up the altar and begun the prescribed religious observances. They and possibly Sheshbazzar (see Ezra 5.16) then laid the foundations of the Temple itself amid great rejoicing. This was the cue for the local opposition and the work had to stop until a ruling could be obtained from Babylon. Cambyses (not Artaxerxes as the Book of Ezra says) would be on the throne and his reply ordered that the building work should stop because of the past reputation of the Jews as a rebellious and seditious people. But Haggai the prophet and Zechariah, the latter not being mentioned in our ritual, persuaded Zerubbabel and Joshua to press ahead with the work and when they were challenged by the local governor they referred him to the decree of Cyrus. By this time we are told that the Temple 'is builded with great stones, and timber is laid upon the walls, and the work goeth fast on and prospereth in their hands'[1]. A search in the royal archives was ordered and the original decree found at which the king, now Darius, sanctioned the completion of the building (and here I quote from the translation of the decree as given in the Bible) 'the foundations thereof [to be] strongly laid; the height thereof threescore cubits and the breadth thereof threescore cubits; with three rows of great stones and a row of new timber'[2]. He also gave orders for the return to Jerusalem of the remaining vessels taken from the Temple by Nebuchadnezzar and for all necessary assistance to be given to finish the building. This time there was no dispute and the work was completed in the sixth year of his reign, about 516 BC,.some twenty years after it had been started. As you will see, all the toing and froing had taken up a great deal of time.

Where, you may well ask, were Ezra and Nehemiah in all this? The answer is somewhat surprising to anyone steeped in our ritual but without much knowledge about the history of the period, for neither of them appear for another twenty years. Ezra was sent to Jerusalem, probably in 458 BC by Artaxerxes who reigned from 464 to 423 BC. His mission was 'to enquire concerning Judah and Jerusalem, according to the law of the Lord thy God which is in thine hand'[3]. He was learned in that law, a staunch upholder of the customs and edicts of the Jewish religion, descendant of a High Priest, said to have been prevented by his studies from going back to Jerusalem earlier. He may have been motivated by the longing to return that was so formidable a trait of the Jewish character, but it is likely that he was also alarmed at rumours that all was not well there, that worship in the Temple was already being neglected and that alien customs were being allowed to corrupt the purity of the law and of the Jewish blood. He was armed with an imperial firman and lost no time in convincing the people of their errors and re-establishing a strict observance of the law by both priests and people. The enthusiasm of the early days of the return does not seem to have been long-lasting, nor indeed were his own reforms.

Later, perhaps even as late as 444 BC, Nehemiah, who also came from the court of Artaxerxes, was moved by sorrow at a report of trouble at Jerusalem where the walls had again been broken down and the gates burned. He obtained a letter from the king, who was at the palace at Susa about 250 miles east of Babylon, authorizing him to go to Jerusalem and effect repairs. On his arrival he arranged for the speedy rebuilding of the walls by men with the trowel in the hand and the sword by the side, a necessity which emphasizes the unsettled state of the country[4].

Now it is time to look at our legend of the Sojourners which seems to be found only in masonic tradition. We must remember that the Royal Arch as a degree seems to have been invented in the eighteenth century; it has of course a biblical base for its legend though not, as we have seen, one that was in all respects historically accurate even in biblical terms. Whether it drew upon old legend or not we cannot say, though no legend has been found with satisfactorily accounts for all its facets. However, we know that there had been persistent rumours that the holy treasures had not been lost when the Temple had been destroyed by Nebuchadnezzar. In the second book of Maccabees in the Apocrypha, written at least 300 years later than the first return from the captivity and many years after Alexander the Great had overthrown the Persian empire, we are told that when the destruction of Jerusalem by the Assyrians was imminent, the prophet Jeremiah (or Jeremy as the Authorised Version of the Bible has it at this point) took the Tabernacle, the Ark of the Covenant and the Altar of incense from the Temple and (here I quote) 'went forth into the mountain where Moses climbed up and saw the heritage of God. And when Jeremy came thither, he found an hollow cave, wherein he laid the tabernacle, and the ark, and the altar of incense, and so stopped the door. And some of those that followed him came to mark the way, but they could not find it. Which when Jeremy perceived, he blamed them, saying, As for that place, it shall be unknown until the time that God gather his people again together, and receive them unto mercy'[5].

That then is one legend; another, also given in Maccabees, concerns the fire from the altar[6]. According to this, the priests took the fire from the altar and hid it 'in an hollow place of a pit without water, where they kept it sure, so that the place was unknown to all men'. It is related that Nehemiah sent descendants of the priests to recover the fire; they found the pit full of thick water which he ordered them to sprinkle on the sacrifices on the altar and when the sun shone on it (here again I quote) 'there was a great fire kindled, so that every man marvelled', as well as they might.

So there you have two legends, one of the hiding of the Ark, Tabernacle and Altar in a cave and the other of a hidden crypt. The legend of the Sojourners relates of course to earlier days, when king Solomon built the first Temple; and those who are Cryptic Masons and aware of the masonic tradition of how the secrets came to be where they were later found, will recognize similarities with these Apocrypha legends — the existence of some hidden repository and the burying of sacred treasures. We are not alone in having a tradition that action was taken to preserve the treasures of the first Temple.

Where our tradition differs is over the deposit and discovery, and frankly I prefer the version we have, not as historically more credible but as a more coherent, natural and meaningful narrative. Although the Royal Arch is almost certainly an invented Degree, invention in such matters is usually the child of necessity and speculation. The third degree as we know it presents an incomplete narrative, impressive in narration but unsatisfying in content because it poses more questions than it answers. More was necessary, the rumours were there and the degree was born. Even though it is difficult to unravel fact and fiction, nevertheless it has a very important lesson to teach.

Think about it. The Sojourners came from Babylon, from a great and glorious city. They arrived at Jerusalem, the city of legend, a place of which their fathers had been telling them tales of wonder; and they found only desolation, deserted ruins, piles of rubble, a vivid reminder of the disobedience to God that had led to their exile in a foreign land. Small wonder they were content to be employed in a menial task.

So they toiled, dutifully clearing away the rubbish until one day they came upon carving so lovely that they paused and then went on with great care, uncovering first one, then another pillar 'of exquisite beauty and symmetry' with a way between them. They ordered their work to follow the path they had found and it led them past yet more pillars until at last they stood beneath the site of the Holy of Holies; and then — nothing. Only solid rock. In his disappointment and frustration one banged the ground with his crowbar and it met the earth with a hollow sound. They looked again and found they were standing on worked stone. The vault was opened and the treasures were found.

Here we have an example of the constant contrast between Craft and Royal Arch, that between the ephemeral and the eternal. When the ground was opened by the trusty Fellow Crafts in the Craft legend they found a dead body; when the Sojourners opened the vault they found an altar to God and the Ineffable Name. Search the ritual and you will find many such contrasts, all stressing the way in which the Royal Arch puts the teaching of the Craft into the context of eternity. That is why the Chapter is important and indeed necessary — the Craft alone is not enough. The Royal Arch is to the Craft as Jerusalem became to Babylon.

After the reign of Solomon the powers of the earth had overwhelmed the Jews. Ten of the twelve tribes disappeared; the other two were hemmed in by enemies and eventually lost all their wordly possessions, even their homes and their Temple. But it was not the end of the story. Earthly power, disappointment and frustration never are. That is one lesson which the historical outline I have been sketching for you teaches us. The Temple was destroyed but the crypt with its secrets survived. The Royal Arch by its legend calls on us to pin our faith on things eternal according as each is taught by his religion. Of course we have to be mindful also of our duties here on earth as we are taught them in the Craft. Some years ago RW Brother Baillieu said in an address in Australia 'I am convinced that Masonry requires from us a positive and not a passive role. To be worthy of our principles we must do something in the short span allowed to us to improve the society in which we live; we cannot properly sit back and leave the task to others'[7]. Those words emphasize that each of us has his part to play in ensuring that our fraternity develops and advances for the benefit of mankind in general as much as for Freemasonry in particular. But the Royal Arch teaches us that as the grandeur, the perils and the struggles of this world, which seem so important now, grow meaningless with time and pass as the glory of Solomon's Temple and the captivity of his people both passed, so too do disappointment and frustration fade as we realize that there is a meaning to life because we are creatures of a Creator Who has His purpose for each of us and Whom it is our bounden duty to revere in accordance with the teachings of religion, however we may worship and whatever the individual's religious belief. In final analysis the legend of the Craft is one of failure and loss, a story of the victory of mortality. The Royal Arch transforms that legend and its teaching by placing them in a framework of eternity and so gives them perspective and meaning within the context of religion. That is the great lesson and the reason why it is the completion of our system. Babylon is now only a heap of rubble: but Jerusalem has survived.

[1] *Ezra* 5; 8.
[2] *Ezra* 6: 3, 4.
[3] *Ezra* 7: 14.
[4] See *Nehemiah*,4: 16-18.
[5] *Maccabees* II,2: 4-7.
[6] *Maccabees* II 1: 19-22.
[7] Speech in March 1979 to Grand Lodge of New South Wales, printed in minutes of Quarterly Communication, United Grand Lodge of England, 25 April 1979, Appendix 'B'. The quotation is at p.417.

A FINAL WORD

The documents which have formed this book all originated as addresses and I have not tried to change that format. Consequently they can be suitable for delivery as talks in Chapter, and if any Companion of the Order wishes to use any of them in that way he has my full permission to do so subject of course (for reasons not of pride but of copyright) to acknowledging their source before beginning. If they are found useful in this way the effort of preparing them for publication will be amply repaid; and as all royalties from sales are devoted to the Benevolent Fund for the Province of Northamptonshire and Huntingdonshire it would be a kindly acknowledgement if when one is used by a Chapter a suitable contribution were to be made to that Fund.

RSES 1990

Appendix A
What is Freemasonry
Leaflet Published by the United Grand Lodge of England

Freemasonry is one of the world's oldest secular fraternal societies. This leaflet is intended to explain Freemasonry as it is practised under the United Grand Lodge of England, which administers Lodges of Freemasons in England and Wales and in many places overseas. The explanation may correct some misconceptions.

Freemasonry is a society of men concerned with moral and spiritual values. Its members are taught its precepts by a series of ritual dramas, which follow ancient forms and use stonemasons' customs and tools as allegorical guides.

The Essential Qualification for Membership

The essential qualification for admission into and continuing membership is a belief in a Supreme Being.

Membership is open to men of any race or religion who can fulfil this essential qualification and are of good repute.

Freemasonry and Religion

Freemasonry is not a religion, nor is it a substitute for religion. Its essential qualification opens it to men of many religions and it expects them to continue to follow their own faith. It does not allow religion to be discussed at its meetings.

The Three Great Principles

For many years Freemasons have followed three great principles:

Brotherly Love

Every true Freemason will show tolerance and respect for the opinions of others and behave with kindness and understanding to his fellow creatures.

Relief

Freemasons are taught to practise charity, and to care, not only for their own, but also for the community as a whole, both by charitable giving, and by voluntary efforts and works as individuals.

Truth

Freemasons strive for truth, requiring high moral standards and aiming to achieve them in their own lives.

Freemasons believe that these principles represent a way of achieving higher standards in life.

Charity

From its earliest days, Freemasonry has been concerned with the care of orphans, the sick and the aged. This work continues today. In addition, large sums are given to national and local charities.

Freemasonry and Society

Freemasonry demands from its members a respect for the law of the country in which a man works and lives.

Its principles do not in any way conflict with its members' duties as citizens, but should strengthen them in fulfilling their public and private responsibilities.

The use by a Freemason of his membership to promote his own or anyone else's business, professional or personal interests is condemned, and is contrary to the conditions on which he sought admission to Freemasonry.

His duty as a citizen must always prevail over any obligation to other Freemasons, and any attempt to shield a Freemason who has acted dishonourably or unlawfully is contrary to this prime duty.

Secrecy

The secrets of Freemasonry are concerned with its traditional modes of recognition. It is not a secret society, since all members are free to acknowledge their membership and will do so in response to inquiries for respectable reasons. Its constitutions and rules are available to the public. There is no secret about any of its aims and principles. Like many other societies, it regards some of its internal affairs as private matters for its members.

Freemasonry and Politics

Freemasonry is non-political, and the discussion of politics at Masonic meetings is forbidden.

Other Masonic Bodies

Freemasonry is practised under many independent Grand Lodges with standards similar to those set by the United Grand Lodge of England.

There are some Grand Lodges and other apparently masonic bodies which do not meet these standards, e.g. which do not require a belief in a Supreme Being, or which allow or encourage their members as such to participate in political matters. These Grand Lodges and bodies are not recognised by the United Grand Lodge of England as being masonically regular, and masonic contact with them is forbidden.

Conclusion

A Freemason is encouraged to do his duty first to his God (by whatever name he is known) through his faith and religious practice; and then, without detriment to his family and those dependent on him, to his neighbour through charity and service.

None of these ideas is exclusively Masonic, but all should be universally acceptable. Freemasons are expected to follow them.

Appendix B

Extract From 'Freemasonry and Christianity' (1987)

'112 These questions need to be considered in the context of contemporary interest in and experiment with inter-faith services. Only last year, the Bishop of Rome himself(*) was in Assisi praying for peace alongside Buddhists, Sikhs, Jews, and medicine men of North American Indian tribes. When he listened attentively to their prayers was he joining in them or unobtrusively dissociating himself from what was going on? Was the whole affair, in which the Archbishop of Canterbury was himself prominent, just an exhibition of spiritual sleight-of-hand or ecclesiatical hyprocrisy?'

i.e., His Holiness the Pope.

Appendix C
'Relationship of Masonry and Religion'

Adopted by United Grand Lodge 12 September 1962, and affirmed 9 December 1981.

'The Board of General Purposes has been giving the most earnest consideration to this subject, being convinced that it is of fundamental importance to the reputation and well-being of English Freemasonry that no misunderstanding should exist inside or outside the Craft.

'It cannot be too strongly asserted that Masonry is neither a religion nor a substitute for religion. Masonry seeks to inculcate in its members a standard of conduct and behaviour which it believes to be acceptable to all creeds, but studiously refrains from intervening in the field of dogma or theology. Masonry, therefore, is not a competitor with religion though in the sphere of human conduct it may be hoped that its teaching will be complementary to that of religion. On the other hand its basic requirement that every member of the Order shall believe in a Supreme Being and the stress laid upon his duty towards Him should be sufficient evidence to all but the wilfully prejudiced that Masonry is an upholder of religion since it both requires a man to have some form of religious belief before he can be admitted as a Mason, and expects him when admitted to go on practising his religion.'

Appendix D
Freemasonry and Religion
Leaflet published by The United Grand Lodge of England

Introduction

This leaflet is intended to deal with a topic mentioned in the leaflet 'What is Freemasonry'. It explains the United Grand Lodge of England's view of the relationship between Freemasonry and Religion.

Basic statement

Freemasonry is not a religion, nor is it a substitute for religion. It demands of its members a belief in a Supreme Being but provides no system of faith of its own.

Freemasonry is open to men of all religious faiths. The discussion of religion at its meetings is forbidden.

The Supreme Being

The names used for the Supreme Being enable men of different faiths to join in prayer (to God as each sees Him) without the terms of the prayer causing dissension among them.

There is no separate Masonic God; a Freemason's God remains the God of the religion he professes.

Freemasons meet in common respect for the Supreme Being as He remains Supreme in their individual religions, and it is no part of Freemasonry to attempt to join religions together. There is therefore no composite Masonic God.

Volume of the Sacred Law

The Holy Bible, referred to by Freemasons as the Volume of the Sacred Law, is always open at every Masonic meeting.

The Obligations of Freemasonry

The obligations taken by Freemasons are sworn on or involve the Volume of the Sacred Law, or the book held sacred by those concerned. They are undertakings to help keep secret a Freemason's means of recognition, and to follow the principles of Freemasonry.

The physical penalties are purely symbolic. The commitment to follow the principles of Freemasonry is, however, deep.

Freemasonry compared with Religion

Freemasonry lacks the basic elements of religion:
a. It has no theological doctrine, and by forbidding religious discussion at its meetings will not allow a Masonic theological doctrine to develop.
b. It offers no sacraments.
c. It does not claim to lead to salvation by works, by secret knowledge or by any other means. The secrets of Freemasonry are concerned with modes of recognition and not with salvation.

Freemasonry supports Religion

Freemasonry is far from indifferent to religion. Without interfering in religious practice it expects each member to follow his own faith, and to place above all other duties his duty to God by whatever name He is known. Its moral teachings are acceptable to all religions.

Freemasonry is thus a supporter of religion.